SURFING THE INTERNET
THEN, NOW, LATER.

SURFING THE INTERNET,
THEN, NOW, LATER.

ISBN: 978-1-291-77653-9

SURFING THE INTERNET,
THEN, NOW, LATER.

ISBN: 978-1-291-77653-9

1

SURFING THE INTERNET
THEN, NOW, LATER.

CONTENTS   **PAGE:**

ANDREAS SOFRONIOU

SURFING THE INTERNET
THEN, NOW, LATER.

SURFING THE INTERNET
THEN, NOW, LATER.

4

ANDREAS SOFRONIOU

SURFING THE INTERNET
THEN, NOW, LATER.

ANDREAS SOFRONIOU

SURFING THE INTERNET
THEN, NOW, LATER.

1. SURFING IN CYBERSPACE

1.1 FICTION AND REALITY

Like the Land of Oz, cyberspace was originally the invention of a writer, the science-fiction novelist William Gibson. While Oz remains the domain of a wizard and a little girl from Kansas, however, cyberspace has leapt off the page to become a subject of wide public interest and debate. As both a dream and a reality, it has sparked renewed discussion about the social and economic assumptions underlying our present means of communication, as well as the role of technology in our lives. By the beginning of 1995, there was a growing consensus that cyberspace had become a region that could significantly affect the structure of our economies, the development of our communities, and the protection of our rights as free citizens.

1.2 NOVELS

Gibson's cyberspace, as described in his book Neuromancer (1984) and several later novels, was an artificial environment created by computers. Unlike a motion picture, which presents moving images on a flat surface, a cyberspatial environment would convey realistic detail in three dimensions and to all five senses. It would also allow for a degree of face-to-face intimacy between people in remote places. In one of Gibson's novels, for instance, a woman "meets" a mysterious financier outside a cathedral in Barcelona, Spain, though in fact she is sitting alone in an office in Brussels. Research continues into ways of realizing this type of cyberspatial experience, which has come to be known as virtual reality. By 1994 virtual reality machines had begun to appear in amusement parks and shopping malls, though a full experience of Gibson's vision has so far been frustrated by the crude state of the technology and by the physical disorientation, bordering on nausea, that some machines provoke. Moreover, users of virtual reality devices are usually communicating not with others but only with the computer.

ANDREAS SOFRONIOU

1.3 CYBERSPACE AND NETWORKS

Cyberspace as a present reality has come to be associated primarily with networks of computers linked through telephone lines. The biggest and most familiar of these, the Internet, was developed in the 1970s to assist U.S. military and academic research. As recently as 1990, the Internet was almost unknown to the general public. By the end of 1995, however, the network had absorbed millions of users with no affiliations to defence institutions or universities. The volume of exchanges between these users, who numbered at least 20 million-30 million in 1995, surpassed 30 terabytes per month, or enough information to fill 30 million books of 700 pages each. For many of those involved in these exchanges--and for millions more who have no experience of computer networks--cyberspace and the Internet have become nearly synonymous terms.

1.4 HYBRID MEDIUM

The Internet is a hybrid medium, combining aspects of the printing press, the telephone, the public bulletin board, and the private letter. It also permits crude radio and television transmission without the physical plant required by conventional broadcasting. Indeed, some commentators have predicted that the Internet or a successor network will eventually absorb the functions of television, telephone, and conventional publishing. They speak of an "information superhighway," a term coined in 1992 by then senator Al Gore, Jr., to refer to a unified, interactive system of electronic communication.

The prospect of such a system, with the capacity to deliver an unprecedented range of informational services to the home, school, or office, has provoked a flurry of strategic alliances between major commercial interests in the telephone, software-programming, and entertainment industries. By 1995 the business world was beginning to regard the largely non-commercial Internet as the electronic equivalent of China: a huge, ever-growing, and virtually untapped market.

1.5 SOCIAL IMPLICATIONS

For some commentators, however, the social implications of cyberspace far outstrip its commercial potential. Unlike television, which beams its messages to a passive and isolated audience, the Internet depends upon its users to supply and share content and to act cooperatively to aid its dispersal. Since resource sharing and mutual aid are age-old traits of successful social groupings, some Internet advocates argue that the medium may help repair a social fabric badly weakened by television. They claim that cyberspace encourages the formation of "virtual communities," without hindrance from national or geographic boundaries. They also view the Internet as the harbinger of a renaissance in free speech. Since the network gives everyone the tools to become a publisher, they say, cyberspace offers a potent means of freeing public discourse from the control of private newspaper companies and broadcasters.

1.6 ELECTRONIC MEDIUM

Similarly optimistic predictions have greeted the appearance of every major electronic medium, including the telephone, radio, and television. Often, announcements of the new utopia have proved less correct than the statements of dissenting voices. One of the earliest and most prescient warnings about electronic media was delivered by Fedor Dostoyevsky in his novel The Brothers Karamazov (1879-80). "We are assured that the world is becoming more and more united, is being formed into brotherly communion, by the shortening of distances, by the transmitting of thoughts through the air," he wrote. In the novelist's view, however, the devices responsible for these transmissions would only stimulate "meaningless and foolish desires." Dostoyevsky's novel was published only about four years after Alexander Graham Bell secured his patent on the telephone, which may be regarded as the first instrument of cyberspace.

1.7 DISPARITIES

More recent critics have warned that electronic networks, far from creating a true global village, will only exaggerate disparities between rich and poor. Users may turn away from their television sets only to withdraw into narrow communion with other residents of their exclusive "cyburbia." Other commentators have warned of the danger lurking in the great potential for violations of civil and privacy rights through the use of computer networks. As citizens perform more social and commercial transactions in cyberspace, it becomes easier to track their spending habits, private interests, and political beliefs.

1.8 PROTECTION

Advocacy groups such as the Electronic Frontier Foundation have called for vigorous protection of privacy rights in cyberspace. The U.S. government has proposed that a device known as the Clipper Chip be accepted as a standard means for encrypting and decoding messages on the Internet, which would thus protect privacy. Critics observe, however, that the Clipper Chip would feature a "back door" to which the government would retain the only key, allowing it to intercept and decode private messages at will.

1.9 LAWS

Further debate has surrounded the issue of how existing laws affect cyberspace as a public space. A University of Michigan student who published on the Internet a violent rape fantasy in which he named a fellow classmate as his victim was arrested in 1995 by the FBI on suspicion of using interstate communications to threaten another person with injury or kidnap. The charge was eventually dismissed on the grounds that the student's writing did not constitute a threat to do real harm. Some observers regarded the case as an awkward application of a law designed for other, more private media. Fear of a flood of pornographic material cascading onto the screens of young Internet users gripped many a politician and journalist in 1995, even though pornographic images represented less than one-half of one percent of all images on the Internet. Some U.S. legislators proposed new laws requiring strict screening of unregulated computer networks for pornographic materials--a measure critics contended would be comparable to asking telephone companies to monitor their lines for discussions that may assist criminal activity.

1.10 COPYRIGHT

Perhaps the thorniest legal issue of all is that of copyright, which forbids unauthorized duplication of another's original work. The mere act of viewing a document on the Internet, however, offends against this principle since the document is literally copied to the viewer's screen. If the document is then copied onto a storage device such as a floppy disk, the viewer may alter the document and republish it in a form that may not be readily distinguishable from the work of the original author. Some writers and artists have greeted this situation as a new impetus for collective creativity, but for defenders of intellectual property rights it is a problem of unprecedented scale. Some have suggested that the very notion of copyright, which was unknown before the invention of printing, may not survive the advent of cyberspace.

1.11 HUMANS AND TECHNOLOGY

The most intriguing aspect of cyberspace, however, may have more to do with the evolving relationship of humankind with its technologies. At the root of Gibson's notion of computer-simulated worlds and electronically assisted experience is the prospect of a meeting of machine and human at a near-organic level. Some commentators have spoken of a coming "bionic convergence" through which we may all someday be fitted with computer implants that shunt messages directly to and from our brains and that may have the capacity to stimulate electronically our creativity or our response to pleasure. At that level of cyberspatial experience, to borrow a phrase from media theorist Marshall McLuhan, "man becomes, as it were, the sex organs of the machine world." Whether we shall be content with that status, if indeed it becomes ours, remains to be seen.

1.12 TOP OF FORM

Unlike most computer terms, "cyberspace" does not have a standard, objective definition. Instead, it is used to describe the virtual world of computers. For example, an object in cyberspace refers to a block of data floating around a computer system or network. With the advent of the Internet, cyberspace now extends to the global network of computers. So, after sending an e-mail to your friend, you could say

11

you sent the message to her through cyberspace. However, use this term sparingly, as it is a popular newbie term and is well overused.

1.13 NEUROMANCER

The word "cyberspace" is credited to William Gibson, who used it in his book, Neuromancer, written in 1984. Gibson defines cyberspace as "a consensual hallucination experienced daily by billions of legitimate operators, in every nation, by children being taught mathematical concepts... A graphical representation of data abstracted from the banks of every computer in the human system. Unthinkable complexity. Lines of light ranged in the non-space of the mind, clusters and constellations of data"

1.14 LITERATURE AND CINEMA

Cyberspace is a word that began in science fiction literature and cinema in the 1980s, was widely adopted during the subsequent years by computer professionals as well as hobbyists, and became a household term in the 1990s. During this period, the uses of the internet, networking, and digital communication were all growing dramatically and the term "cyberspace" was able to represent the many new ideas and phenomena that were emerging.[1]

1.15 CYBERNETICS

The parent term of cyberspace is "cybernetics", derived from the Ancient Greek κυβερνήτης (kybernētēs, steersman, governor, pilot, or rudder), a word introduced by Norbert Wiener for his pioneering work in electronic communication and control science.

1.16 SOCIAL EXPERIENCE

As a social experience, individuals can interact, exchange ideas, share information, provide social support, conduct business, direct actions, create artistic media, play games, engage in political discussion, and so on, using this global network. They are sometimes referred to as cybernauts. The term cyberspace has become a conventional means to describe anything associated with the Internet and the diverse Internet culture. The United States government recognizes the interconnected information technology and the interdependent network of information technology infrastructures operating across this medium as part of the US national critical infrastructure.

1.17 CYBERETHICS

Amongst individuals on cyberspace, there is believed to be a code of shared rules and ethics mutually beneficial for all to follow, referred to as cyberethics. Many view the right to privacy as most important to a functional code of cyberethics. Such moral responsibilities go hand in hand when working online with global networks, specifically, when opinions are involved with online social experiences.

1.18 SOCIAL INTERACTIONS

According to Chip Morningstar and F. Randall Farmer, cyberspace is defined more by the social interactions involved rather than its technical implementation.[4] In their view, the computational medium in cyberspace is an augmentation of the communication channel between real people; the core characteristic of cyberspace is that it offers an environment that consists of many participants with the ability to affect and influence each other. They derive this concept from the observation that people seek richness, complexity, and depth within a virtual world.

2. SUBJECTS RELATED TO THE INTERNET

2.1 COMPUTERS

A computer is a device for storing and processing data, according to a program of instructions stored within the computer itself. The term computer normally refers to electronic digital computers, but analogue computers also exist for use in specialist applications. Computers are 'universal' information-processing machines: any information-processing task that can be specified by an algorithm (a well-defined sequence of instructions) can, in principle, be performed by a computer. Unlike most other machines, it is not necessary to build a new computer for each new task. Computers can therefore perform a very large number of useful tasks, although limits do exist: it can be proved that some problems are incomputable. The mathematical study of what tasks are capable of being computed is known as compatibility, and complexity is the study of how hard it is to compute a task. Numerical analysis concerns the fastest and most accurate way to solve numerical problems.

2.2 DIGITAL COMPUTER

The digital computer is one of the most significant innovations of the 20th century (see computer, history of). In the four decades since its introduction it has had an impact on almost all areas of human activity (see information technology). Computers are very widely used commercially for data processing and for information storage and retrieval. Manufacturing industry has been affected by developments such as computer-integrated manufacture, and robotics. Much scientific research has been transformed by the ability to analyse large quantities of numerical data and by the use of simulation techniques to model complex systems such as nuclear reactors and the weather. Many technical advances, such as space travel and advanced aircraft design, would have been impossible without the processing ability of computers. Digital computers are available in a very wide range of powers, sizes, and costs, suitable for different applications. Advances in technology have led to rapid improvements in the performance of all types of computer systems: many personal computers are now more powerful than much larger, mainframe computers of the 1960s.

14

2.3 SYSTEMS

A computer system can be regarded as being organized in a number of layers. The lowest layer is the hardware (the physical components of the system, as opposed to the software, the programs and other operating information used by the computer). Both the information which is being processed (the data) and the processing instructions (the program) are stored in the form of bits of information in a memory. The memory unit is connected by a bus to the central processing unit (CPU), which is the other essential hardware component. The CPU takes one instruction at a time from the memory, decodes it, and then performs the action specified by the instruction. Each instruction specifies a very simple operation, for example, multiplying together two numbers or checking that two pieces of information are identical.

2.4 PERIPHERALS

Other hardware items are peripheral devices, which include permanent data storage devices such as hard and floppy disks, input devices for feeding information into the system, and output devices through which results are fed out. A small layer of software above the hardware, called the microcode, allows the computer to execute a larger set of instructions than could be easily provided in hardware alone. The hardware and the microcode together execute machine code.

2.5 SOFTWARE

The next layer in the computer's organization is a much larger body of software, the operating system. It interprets additional, very complex instructions which allow reading from and writing to files, input devices, and output devices. The layer above this is provided by the compiler or interpreter, which allows a programmer to write programs in a problem-orientated computer language, rather than in machine code or assembly language. The programmer working with such a language needs to know nothing of the layers below, so that a FORTRAN programmer can regard any computer with a FORTRAN compiler as if it were with a FORTRAN machine.

15

2.6 APPLICATIONS

The final layer of software comprises the computer's applications programs. Computing is about the correct design and implementation of useful applications programs from a given specification. Techniques of software engineering are being developed which make specification, design, and implementation a less error-prone process. Mathematics and formal reasoning are used to prove logically that the implementation of computer systems correspond to their specifications. Improving the reliability of programs is increasingly important as their use in safety-critical situations grows. Some large computer programs have many millions of instructions, each instruction being a separate 'working part' that must function correctly. On this basis, computer programs are the most complex artefacts built by humans. The major challenges of computing in the future are the development of software engineering techniques, very high-level computer languages, and parallel processing

2.7 COMPUTER ARCHITECTURE

Computer architecture is the design and structure of the hardware components of computer systems. The term embraces general considerations, such as whether a system is based on serial, parallel, or distributed computing, in which several computers are linked together. It also covers more detailed aspects, such as a description of the internal structure of a central processing unit (CPU). A micro-computer is often described as having an 8-bit, 16-bit, or 32-bit architecture according to the length of data word that can be processed by the CPU and the width of the data bus.

2.8 COMPUTER CRIME

This is a crime in which a computer is either a tool of crime or is the object of crime. Using a computer as a tool of crime often involves altering, deleting, or adding to data stored on it. Computer crime is growing because valuable data are stored on computers and it is impossible to maintain absolute security around a computer system, particularly a large one with many users. Electronic banking systems are the commonest target, and industrial espionage involving computers is also becoming a serious threat. Using the 'salami technique', for example, the criminal may illegitimately and regularly transfer funds from many bank accounts but in such small amounts that those defrauded do not notice. Industrial espionage cases often involve illegal access to computer files or networks to obtain confidential information.

2.9 VIRUSES

A computer is the object of crime when it is sabotaged through the planting of computer 'viruses'--for instance, viruses may hold the threat of destroying the databases of large organizations unless money is paid. Viruses are designed to replicate themselves and may lie dormant and undetected within computer systems for some time, and can be passed from system to system without the knowledge of the users. The increase in the use of computers has resulted in legislation against computer crime in many countries, but detecting and proving offences is difficult and many organizations are unwilling publicly to admit that they are victims.

2.10 CYBERNETICS

Cybernetics (from the Greek, kubernetes, steersman) is the study of communication and control systems in machines, animals, and organizations. The discipline developed immediately after World War II, when control-systems and systems-engineering techniques were applied successfully to certain neurological problems. The term cybernetics was first applied in English by Wiener. Cybernetics is characterized by a concentration on the flow of information (rather than energy or material) within a system, and on the use of feedback or 'goal-directed activity' in both technological artefacts and living organisms. Major areas of cybernetic study have been biological control systems, automation, animal communication, and artificial intelligence (AI). The recent rapid expansion of AI as a subject area, together with the development of knowledge-based systems and neural networks, have renewed interest in the general cybernetic approach, although the term 'cybernetics' itself is now rarely used.

2.11 INFORMATION TECHNOLOGY

Information technology (IT) is the umbrella term used to describe the practical applications of computer systems. The term has become prevalent with the increasing use of computers such as word processors for office systems, but it also embraces the more traditional areas of data processing and information retrieval. Key factors in the recent rapid spread of microelectronics and information technology (often known simply as 'new technology') have been the drastic reduction in electronic hardware costs during the 1970s and 1980s; the so-called 'convergence' of computing and telecommunications (sometimes denoted by the term telematics); and the emergence of various formal standards and informal agreements within the IT industry.

2.12 MICROPROCESSORS

The mass production of microprocessors and other electronic components at low unit cost has made it possible to incorporate digital electronics into a wide range of products for commerce, industry, and the home. New technology has made an enormous impact on the design and performance of consumer goods, for example, cameras, video and hi-fi equipment, and personal computers. In offices and business, new technology was introduced for text processing, using dedicated (special-purpose) word processors. Now, however, it is usual to find general-purpose small computers and workstations being exploited for a much wider range of office applications using special-purpose application software such as financial planning packages, management support software, information storage and retrieval applications, desk-top publishing, and so on. Expert systems using artificial intelligence techniques to aid decision-making can also be run on suitable personal computers.

2.13 NETWORKS

The combination of computing with private and public telecommunication networks has been particularly significant in retailing and banking. Bar codes on products can be read automatically at check-outs, and the information used both to print a

18

customer's receipt and to reorder necessary stocks. Electronic funds transfer using an 'intelligent' cash register or point-of-sale terminal can then complete the cycle of electronic information flow by automatically debiting the customer's bank or credit-card account by the appropriate amount. Sales records held by the store's central computer can be used to develop overall retailing strategies; records of the purchasing patterns of particular customers can be exploited for direct marketing of goods or services.

2.14 INDUSTRIES

The IT revolution has been just as great in the manufacturing and processing industries. An early application was the numerical control of machine-tools, in which digital electronics were used to control lathes and other equipment. Now it has become common for a wide range of industrial equipment (sensors, control systems, robots, and so on) to incorporate microelectronics and to be interconnected (networked) so that information can be gathered, communicated, and processed in order to optimize the activity. Artificial intelligence, in which computer programs mimic certain aspects of human behaviour, is beginning to play a role in areas such as process control, as well as in mechatronic products combining aspects of electronic, mechanical, and software engineering. Again, the convergence of telecommunications and computing has been a vital factor, allowing the computer to become fully integrated into the manufacturing or other processes (see computer-integrated manufacturing), thus transcending individual applications such as computer-aided design.

2.15 WORKING PRACTICES

The introduction of new technology into areas which have not traditionally used computers has had a great influence on working practices. Some traditional tasks--or even whole categories of tasks-- have disappeared completely and new ones have appeared. In some sectors (printing in the UK, for example), adoption of new technology has led to serious industrial conflict.

2.16 TELECOMMUNICATIONS

Once it became commonplace for information retrieval and data processing to be carried out by digital computers in business and industrial settings, it was also natural for such information to be transmitted digitally using a range of new services; telecommunications has therefore become an essential part of many working environments. Small computers are often linked by means of local area networks within an office or company, so that expensive resources such as laser printers or databases can be shared; a further advantage of such networking is that in-house communication can then include electronic mail, computer conferencing, or even voice messaging, as well as the traditional telephone and memo. Digital telecommunication links extend such facilities to the outside world, providing electronic communication between widely dispersed organizations or individuals, as well as access to external databases or information services.

2.17 WORKING FROM HOME

It is even becoming possible for certain employees to work partially or entirely from home, communicating with colleagues via a computer and modem. In the home, information is available electronically through teletex services such as Ceefax and Oracle as well as call-up videotex such as Prestel. More recently, with a growth in the ownership of home computers, individual users have linked into the Internet. In the future, the combination of telecommunication services (including television), home computer, and new storage media such as videodisc and CD-ROM (see compact disc) is likely to form the core of domestic entertainment and educational applications of IT.

2.18 NEURAL NETWORKS

All the above applications of new technology are based upon a computer architecture which has remained virtually unchanged since the early days of the digital computer. Alternative structures such as neural networks are currently arousing much interest, particularly for their potential in artificial-intelligence applications, while parallel computing offers possibilities for faster processing. In the immediate future, however, further exploitation of new technology is more likely to result from a continuing expansion of telecommunications services and economies of scale in the provision of hardware than from radical changes to computer design. Information technology raises problems of privacy and freedom of information, as data is gathered about citizens who may not have access to records held about them (see data protection, surveillance).

2.19 HISTORY OF COMPUTER

Although the development of the computer has been largely played out during the 20th century, there is a long history of automatic calculation. Hero wrote in the 1st century AD of representing numbers using a train of gears, but little real progress seems to have been made until the early 17th century, when the first calculators were built, and the German mathematician Gottfried Leibniz speculated (1679) on the possibility of building a calculator using moving balls to represent numbers in binary code. The notion of storing a sequence of instructions mechanically is also very old and was incorporated into self-playing musical instruments and other automata even in ancient times. In 1725 Basile Bouchon invented a method of producing intricate woven patterns on a draw loom from instructions on a perforated paper tape. By 1800 this method had been refined by Jacquard into a highly successful automatic loom controlled by punched cards. The idea of punched-card instructions was adapted by Hollerith to record and analyse the results of the 1890 US census in the earliest example of large-scale data processing.

2.20 ANALYTICAL ENGINE

In 1835 Babbage conceived of the basic idea of an analytical engine in which can be found most of the elements of a truly general-purpose computer. He drew together the ideas of mechanical calculation and a set of instructions recorded on perforated paper tape. The development costs of the machine were very high: the British government eventually withdrew funding, and this pioneering machine was never completed. Babbage's ideas were subsequently lost until the 1930s, when work on electromechanical computers was started independently in Germany and the USA.

2.21 STORED PROGRAM

In 1941 Konrad Zuse in Germany built the world's first working stored-program computer. His Z3 machine was based on electromechanical relays, and was used for military aircraft design. In the USA, the mathematician Howard Aiken, in association with IBM (International Business Machines), was working independently on a large electromechanical calculator that could be programmed using paper tape. The Automatic Sequence Controlled Calculator (ASCC), or Harvard Mark I, was completed in 1943; it was very similar in concept (although not in engineering realization), to Babbage's analytical machine.

2.22 THERMIONIC VALVE

Computers based on the electronic thermionic valve were a major development, since they were much faster and more reliable than electromechanical computers. Among the earliest electronic computers were the Colossus series of special-purpose computers, developed secretly in the UK from 1943. They deciphered coded German messages produced on sophisticated mechanical systems called Enigma machines. An important member of the Colossus team was Turing, who in 1936 had published a paper that defined in abstract terms the generalized concept of a universal computer. The concept of the stored-program computer (an idea attributed to von Neumann), in which instructions for processing data are stored along with the data in the computer's own memory, proved to be very important, since it hugely enhanced the flexibility and potential of the computer. The earliest electronic stored-program computer was an experimental machine built under the leadership of Frederick Williams at Manchester University, UK, in 1948. This was followed by the Manchester Mark 1 computer in 1949 which, as the Ferranti Mark 1, was the first commercially available computer to be delivered. Other notable early computers in the UK were EDSAC at Cambridge, later marketed as LEO, and Turing's ACE at the National Physical Laboratory.

22

2.23 TRANSISTOR

Mauchly and Eckert at the University of Pennsylvania (USA) developed the ENIAC and EDVAC computers based on the highly influential ideas of von Neumann; they later developed the successful UNIVAC computer, which became commercially available in 1951. The development of the transistor led to much cheaper, faster, and more reliable computers. The first transistorized computer was working at Manchester University in 1953, although the USA had a number of much larger computers operating within a few years.

2.24 COMPILER

The first compiler was developed at Manchester in 1952, and in 1954 John Backus of IBM in the USA developed FORTRAN, the first internationally used computer language. A significant high point in this era was the joint development of the Atlas computer by Ferranti Ltd. and Manchester University. This was the world's first super-computer, and pioneered many aspects of computer architecture that are common today. After this, most major developments took place in the USA. Particularly crucial was the development of the integrated circuit (IC) in 1958 which allowed complete circuits to be manufactured on a tiny piece of silicon. In 1972 the Intel Corporation developed the world's first microprocessor, the Intel 4004, which was very limited but was an immediate commercial success and led directly to the development of today's cheap, fast, and reliable microcomputer as well as much more powerful mainframe computers

2.25 COMPUTER LANGUAGE

This is a specialized, formal language used to write computer programs. Computer languages were developed to relieve programmers of the arduous task of writing programs directly in machine code. There are two broad classes of conventional programming languages: low-level languages, such as assembly language, in which each instruction represents a single machine code operation, and high-level languages, in which each instruction may represent an operation involving many machine code instructions. In both cases a special program, either an assembler, a compiler, or an

23

interpreter, must be used to translate the source code to machine code before the program can be run on a computer. A job-control language, or command language, is the usual interface between a computer and the operating system. It allows the user to describe what tasks, or jobs, are to be processed by the computer. The system interprets the user's commands and runs the required application programs.

2.26 AUTOCODE. FORTRAN AND COBOL

The Swiss engineer Konrad Zuse is credited with the invention of the first programming language shortly after World War II. AUTOCODE, the first high-level language complete with translation program, was developed at Manchester University, UK, in the early 1950s. Since then hundreds of different programming languages have been designed, but only a few are in widespread use. The first two languages to be widely used (FORTRAN and COBOL) were released around 1957. Both languages dominated their respective fields for the next two decades and are still in widespread use.

2.27 ALGOL AND PASCAL

In 1958 ALGOL was developed by an international committee. Although ALGOL evolved over the next decade it had greater theoretical than practical significance. However, it did spawn PASCAL, one of today's most commonly used languages. BASIC, which was developed in the mid-1960s at Dartmouth College, USA, is the best-known language for programming microcomputers.

2.28 LOGICAL LANGUAGES

Nowadays, the preferred language for much professional program development is C, designed at Bell Laboratories, USA, in 1971 to implement the UNIX operating system. Most artificial intelligence applications use symbolic or logical languages, such as LISP and PROLOG, rather than conventional programming languages.

2.29 TELEPHONY

Telephony is the transmission of speech via an electrical signal between one telephone receiver and another, the signal being transmitted either along a cable or by radio or optical-fibre transmission. Alexander Graham Bell patented the first telephone receiver and transmitter in the UK and the USA during 1876 and demonstrated it in Philadelphia. Transmission between receivers was electrical, along wires, the signal being an exact copy of the sound wave. Telephony quickly developed into a sophisticated communications system over fairly short distances; by 1887 there were over 100,000 telephone subscribers world-wide. Further development took place more slowly. Hard-drawn copper wire soon replaced steel for telephone wires, being a better conductor of electricity. Underground and submarine cables were introduced in cities and for crossing water. Interference between two or more adjacent lines was reduced by using an all-metal (two-wire) circuit instead of one in which the earth was used as a conducting path. Inductors at regular intervals along a telephone line were found to reduce distortion over long distances, and later repeaters, which boosted or amplified the telephone signal, were introduced.

Transatlantic telephone transmission relied on high-frequency radio transmission until 1956, because submarine cable links were not sufficiently reliable.

2.30 SATELLITE LINKS

Communications satellite links using microwaves are now used for many international calls. Optical-fibre cables are a recent introduction; they give virtually noise-free transmission. Another recent development has been the digitization of telephone signals. Digital signals can be multiplexed easily, and pulse code modulation offers a way of transmitting the digital signals with minimal noise or distortion. In addition, such a signal can be strengthened and reshaped en route, and digital signals are in an appropriate form for computer processing. Telephone circuits now also carry telex, fax, electronic mail, and television signals in a form that can be fed directly into appropriate receivers. Additionally, they are used to enable computers to communicate over large distances. As a consequence, telephone systems have become an integral part of modern telecommunications.

2.31 CELLULAR TELEPHONE (MOBILE)

Cellular telephone is a mobile radio telephone communications system. The concept originated at the Bell Telephone Laboratories, USA, during 1947. It was first demonstrated in Chicago during 1977, and initiated in the UK in 1985. The basic system involves dividing the country into areas or cells, 2-13 km (1.25-8 miles) in radius, and employing different frequency bands in neighbouring cells to avoid interference. A mobile caller connects into the national telephone network via radio communication with the telephone exchange in his cell. The mobile units must be able to retune to a new frequency as they pass from one cell to another, a process that demands a highly sophisticated electronic switching system. A digitized network served by satellites is being introduced.

2.32 EXCHANGE OF INFORMATION

Communication is a mutual exchange of information between individuals, a process central to human experience and social organization. The study of communication involves many disciplines, including linguistics, psychology, sociology, and anthropology. All forms of communication, from interpersonal to mass media communications, involve an initiator, who formulates a message and sends it as a signal, by means of a particular channel, to a receiver, who decodes and interprets the meaning. In interpersonal communication involving face-to-face conversation, communication is direct, using the code of language, and reinforced by non-verbal communication such as body movement, eye contact, gesture, and facial expression. Response is also direct. Interpersonal communication can also take place at a distance.

2.33 CONVEYING MESSAGES

Other forms of communication use writing and printing as the means of conveying messages. The invention of the printing press was the first step in the development of mass communication. Books, newspapers, and periodicals are able to convey messages to a wide audience; an even wider audience is reached by radio and television, film, and the recording industries. The mass media and the arts impose their own codes and characteristics on to their messages, which can range from relatively straightforward ideological tracts to complex texts carrying multiple layers of possible meaning.

2.34 TELECOMMUNICATION

Telecommunications are the communication of information (usually audio, visual, or computer data) over a distance, transmitted by various means. Early techniques included signal fires and semaphore; modern systems include telephony, telex, fax radio, television and computer. Over short distances electrical telegraph or telephone signals can be transmitted via two-wire telephone lines without additional processing. For longer distances, various techniques of modulation and/or coding at the transmitter, followed by demodulation or decoding at the receiver, are employed to match the transmitted signal to the properties of the telecommunications channel. Transmission may be to a single receiver or it may be broadcast to many individual receivers; it may be direct or switched through a complex network. Until recently most telecommunications systems were analogue in nature, but now the message signal commonly undergoes digitization at the transmitter, using pulse code modulation or similar techniques: it is then decoded into usable form (sound, print, video, and so on) at the receiver.

2.35 DIGITIZATION

The widespread digitization of telecommunications signals has begun a trend in many countries towards the combination of hitherto separate systems into a single Integrated Services Digital Network (ISDN). It has also resulted in the convergence of computing and telecommunications (see information technology). Because of the complexity of modern telecommunications systems, standardization bodies such as the International Telecommunications Union (ITU), and the International Organization for Standardization (ISO) have taken on great importance, particularly in the design of 'open' systems which can be easily interconnected.

2.36 MONOPOLY SUPPLIER

Traditionally, telecommunications systems were delivered by a monopoly supplier, usually a branch of government concerned with the postal, telephone, and telegraphic services (in Europe, the PTTs). In the USA the American Telephone and Telegraph was privately owned, but was still subject to government regulations. As the traditional forms of telecommunications were challenged by computer-based forms of communication, there were calls for the break-up and deregulation of the old telecommunications monopolies. In 1984 American Telephone and Telegraph, once the largest company in the world, providing four-fifths of the USA's telephones, and nearly all its home and international long-distance services, had its monopoly broken by the government. It was split into twenty-two local telephone companies grouped into seven regional companies. In Japan the huge Nippon Telegraph and Telephone Company faces similar governmental pressure to break up its monopoly. Markets are also being opened up in Australia and New Zealand, but in most of Europe the retention of a minimum provision of telephone services has been preferred to a policy of greater competition and technological innovation.

2.37 SOCIAL TRANSFORMATION

The use of sophisticated telecommunications systems is transforming all aspects of business, political, and social life, bringing different societies closer together, and enabling speedy decisions to be taken.

2.38 NETWORK

Network (in computing) is used for connecting together separate computer systems so that they can exchange data, and sometimes programs. The points at which individual systems are connected to the network are known as nodes. There are two main classes of computer network: broad area (wide area) networks and local area networks (LANs). As the name implies, the nodes of a broad area network may be widely dispersed geographically; in fact the largest networks may extend world-wide. Typically, broad area networks utilize telecommunication channels to provide the connections between computers. Local area networks usually link computers or workstations on the same site via coaxial cables or optical fibres. LANs are often used to share expensive peripherals such as laser printers, or to share a central disk store, known as a file server. Both types of network usually provide electronic mail facilities to enable users to pass messages to each other.

2.39 INDUSTRY DEVELOPMENTS

The computer industry's Internet obsession also fuelled competition. The biggest rivalry in 1996 may well have been the one between software giant Microsoft Corp. and Netscape. In a battle for "mind share" in the Internet market, each company pitted its free Internet browser software against the others. The war between Netscape Navigator and Microsoft Internet Explorer was fought mainly in the reviewers' columns of computer trade journals, and for most consumers choosing a winner was largely subjective. The contest was important to Netscape, which was trying to maintain its lead as the most innovative Internet communications firm as well as its 80% market share, and to Microsoft, which was trying to prove that it had abandoned its reluctance to develop for the on-line world.

2.40 LEGAL BATTLE

The battle became a legal one as well. In August Netscape sent a letter to the U.S. Justice Department accusing Microsoft of deliberately preventing companies such as Netscape from running some types of Internet server software on Microsoft's Windows NT 4.0 Workstation system software. Microsoft responded that the NT Workstation software was not appropriate for the use Netscape intended.

2.41 INTRANET

One of the major new markets for the computer industry in 1996 was the Intranet, an internal company version of the Internet. Intranets allowed workers with PCs to access information from company computers via the same user-friendly browsing software used on the Internet. Corporations that adopted this approach said Intranets simplified employees' work and thus led to higher worker productivity and lower frustration levels.

29

2.42 COMPUTER SECURITY

Computer-security experts continued to worry about on-line hackers who attacked corporate computers. One of the newest trends was the "denial-of-service" attack, in which a series of phony messages were sent to the target computer via the Internet. This kept the computer so busy that legitimate users could not gain access to it. The potential for such attacks was intensified by the ease with which hackers could learn to become attackers. Anyone could learn denial-of-service techniques simply by visiting Web sites that published information of interest to hackers.

2.43 HACKING

Hackers also broke into U.S. government-related computer systems and altered official Web sites operated by the Justice Department (in August), the CIA (in October), and the air force (in December). Although no serious damage was done, it was increasingly apparent that improved security measures would be crucial on the expanding Internet.

2.44 NETWORK COMPUTER

One of the most talked-about new computer products of 1996 was the "network computer," a stripped-down machine intended to replace the limited-function computer terminals used by corporate workers such as bank tellers, retail clerks, and airline ticketing agents. Priced in the range of $700 without a computer screen, the network computer was designed for users who did not need the complexity of a PC and its software. IBM's first such machine, the Network Station, was to use only browsing software for accessing the Internet or an Intranet. Other companies--notably Sun Microsystems, Inc., and Oracle Corp.-- quickly announced their own network computers. To some extent, the network computer threatened to undermine the PC market by providing a lower-cost alternative for some types of work.

2.45 MICROPROCESSOR CHIPS

Intel Corp., which manufactured the microprocessor chips that controlled most PCs, launched a counterattack by declaring that it would make PCs more affordable by lowering the costs of using them in computer networks. For instance, it said it would offer products that made it easier to diagnose PC problems remotely over a network. The aim was to make PCs more competitive with network computers, which were relatively low-maintenance devices.

2.46 MICROSOFT

Windows 95, which was heavily promoted by Microsoft during the summer of 1995, sold 40 million copies in its first 12 months, which made it a success by any standard. Some software companies that wrote programs for Windows 95 had expected even greater sales of the upgraded operating system (OS), however, and were disappointed. Sales were slowest among corporations, which typically were reluctant to replace the previous version of Windows, which seemed to be working well. Most Windows 95 sales were made through the sale of new PCs that came equipped with the software. Another Microsoft product, the Windows NT OS, continued to sell briskly, and analysts estimated that by year's end it would outsell all types of the Unix operating software.

2.47 PERFORMANCE

Meanwhile, the PC increased in power in 1996 to 200-225 MHz, nearly twice the speed of the fastest consumer computer a year earlier. At the same time, next-generation PCs were being developed that would raise performance to the range of entry-level supercomputers, the high-performance machines used in science and industry. Exponential Technology, Inc., demonstrated a 500-MHz microprocessor chip, while Intel planned its model P7 chip, which would process instructions 64 bits at a time rather than 32 bits at a time, as did the microprocessors used in 1996 PCs.

2.48 CHESS

No matter how powerful computers became, the human mind could still withstand their challenge. In February 1996 Russian chess champion Gary Kasparov defeated Deep Blue, an IBM machine touted as the world's best chess computer.

2.49 SUPPLIERS SUFFER

Some traditional computer suppliers suffered in 1996. The year ended with the future of PC industry pioneer Apple Computer, Inc., still in doubt. While the company reported a $25 million profit in the last quarter of its 1996 fiscal year, which ended in late September, its sales declined by almost $700 million compared with the same period a year earlier. In addition, Apple lost more than $800 million during its fiscal year. Gilbert F. Amelio, Apple's chairman since early 1996, was engaged in what was expected to be a three-year corporate turnaround.

2.50 TURNAROUND

The direction of that turnaround took on a new dimension at year's end when Apple, which had been negotiating with Be, Inc., for the use of its Be OS, unexpectedly announced the acquisition of NeXT Software, Inc., for $400 million. The deal also signaled the return to Apple of its cofounder, Steven Jobs, who formed NeXT after being ousted from Apple by the board of directors in a 1985 power struggle. It was uncertain how NeXT's highly regarded but little-used NeXTSTEP OS would be incorporated into a new, more advanced replacement for the aging Macintosh operating system (Mac OS). Jobs would reportedly be a part-time adviser at Apple while continuing in his role as the chief executive at Pixar Animation Studios, which took the world by storm in 1996 with its full-length computer-animated film, Toy Story.

2.51 CLONES

Apple also hoped to get a boost from the decision of Motorola, Inc., which manufactured the PowerPC microprocessor chips used in recent Macintosh computers, to begin making "clones," PCs that would run the Mac OS. Although Apple had previously been reluctant to license the Mac OS, in 1996 licensed clone makers included Power Computing Corp., DayStar Digital, Inc., and the Taiwanese manufacturer Umax Data Systems, Inc.

2.52 TROUBLES AND CONSOLIDATION

Digital Equipment Corp. also continued to be troubled, losing $433 million in the fiscal year ended in mid-1996 and announcing it would eliminate 7,000 jobs. In its following quarter DEC lost another $66 million, disappointing Wall Street with a decline that was far larger than expected.

It also was a year for consolidation in the PC industry. In June U.S. PC manufacturer Packard Bell said it would merge with the PC operations of Japanese computer manufacturer NEC. The $300 million deal would create the largest PC firm in the U.S., which would be headed by Packard Bell management. NEC previously had been a major shareholder in Packard Bell.

2.53 MILLENNIUM BUG

During 1996 government agencies and corporations appeared to be taking a more serious look at the computer problems posed by the approaching end of the century. Because of a flaw in the way some computer programs handled calendar dates; many programs would cease functioning or give wrong answers in the year 2000. For more than 30 years, most computer programmers had been abbreviating calendar-date years as the last two digits--a shortcut that originally served the purpose of saving expensive computer memory capacity but continued as common practice long after computer memory had become relatively cheap. As a result, while all computer programs could recognize that "96" meant 1996, most either could not make sense of the year 2000 abbreviated as "00" or else concluded that it meant 1900. The problem was complicated by the ingenuity of the

33

original computer programmers, who hid date calculations inside programs in clever and unexpected ways and thus made it difficult for modern programmers to locate and change all two-digit dates to four-digit ones. Some analysts calculated that the cost of finding and fixing all "year 2000 problem" flaws would be between $300 billion and $600 billion worldwide by the end of the decade.

In a sense, the year 2000 problem had already arrived by 1996, because forward-looking business programs, such as those that calculated home mortgages or interest or that did sales forecasting, already had bumped up against the year 2000 in their daily tasks. As a result, a mini-industry of year 2000 consulting and programming services was growing up to help corporate and government computer users solve their problems.

2.54 TALENT LOST

The computer industry lost a major talent when computer pioneer Seymour Cray died of injuries suffered in an automobile accident in October 2000.

34

SURFING THE INTERNET
THEN, NOW, LATER.

3. THE INTERNET THEN

3.1 ARPANET

In 1969 the Advanced Research Projects Agency (ARPA) of the U.S. Department of Defence established a data communications network called ARPANET. By using packet-switching techniques, ARPANET connected heterogeneous computers located at universities and military installations anywhere in the United States. It was the first network to use layered protocols, flow control, and fault-tolerance-- exemplified by the fact that a node could disappear without bringing down the entire network or requiring any operator intervention. The word "packet" was coined by ARPANET developers to distinguish between the longer messages generated by computers and the smaller segments used by ARPANET to improve data throughput. The Internet, an outgrowth of ARPANET, connects millions of computers worldwide.

3.2 INTERNET

Internet is a global network that connects other computer networks, together with software and protocols for controlling the movement of data. The Internet, often referred to as 'the Net', stems from a network called ARAPNET (Advanced Research Project Agency Network), which was initiated in 1969 by a group of universities and private research groups funded by the US Department of Defence. It now covers almost every country in the world. Its organization is informal and deliberately non-political -- its controllers tend to concentrate on technical aspects rather than on administrative control.

3.3 BASIC SERVICES

The Internet offers users a number of basic services including data transfer, electronic mail, and the ability to access information in remote databases. A notable feature is the existence of user groups, which allow people to exchange information and debate specific subjects of interest. In addition, there are a number of high-level services. For example, MBONE (multicast backbone service) allows the transmission of messages to more than one destination. It is used in videoconferencing. The World Wide Web, known as 'the Web', is

35

another high-level Internet service, developed in the 1990s at CERN in Geneva. It is a service for distributing multimedia information, including graphics, pictures, sounds, and video as well as text. A feature of the World Wide Web is that it allows links to other related documents elsewhere on the Internet. Documents for publication on the Web are presented in a form known as HTML (hypertext mark-up language). This allows a specification of the page layout and typography as it will appear on the screen. It also allows the inclusion of active links to other documents. Generally, these appear on the screen display as highlighted text or as additional icons. Typically, the user can use a mouse to 'click' on one of these points to load and view a related document. Many commercial and public organizations now have their own Web site (specified by an address code) and publish a 'home page', giving information about the organization.

3.4 ACADEMIC AND RESEARCH ORGANIZATIONS

Up to the mid-1990s, the major users of the Internet were academic and research organizations. This has begun to change rapidly with individual home users linking in through commercial access providers and with a growing interest by companies in using the Internet for publicity, sales, and as a medium for electronic publishing. At the same time, there are problems with the flow of information across national borders, bringing in debates about copyright protection, data protection, the publication of pornography, and ultimately political control and censorship.

3.5 SUMMARISING THE INTERNET

In summarising, the Internet is a network connecting many computer networks and based on a common addressing system and communications protocol called TCP/IP (Transmission Control Protocol/Internet Protocol). From its creation in 1983 it grew rapidly beyond its largely academic origin into an increasingly commercial and popular medium.

By the mid-1990s the Internet connected millions of computers throughout the world. Many commercial computer network and data services also provided at least indirect connection to the Internet.

SURFING THE INTERNET
THEN, NOW, LATER.

The original uses of the Internet were electronic mail (commonly called "E-mail"), file transfer (using ftp, or file transfer protocol), bulletin boards and newsgroups, and remote computer access (telnet). The World Wide Web, which enables simple and intuitive navigation of Internet sites through a graphical interface, expanded dramatically during the 1990s to become the most important component of the Internet.

The Internet had its origin in a U.S. Department of Defense program called ARPANET (Advanced Research Projects Agency Network), established in 1969 to provide a secure and survivable communications network for organizations engaged in defense-related research. Researchers and academics in other fields began to make use of the network, and at length the National Science Foundation (NSF), which had created a similar and parallel network called NSFNet, took over much of the TCP/IP technology from ARPANET and established a distributed network of networks capable of handling far greater traffic. NSF continues to maintain the backbone of the network (which carries data at a rate of 45 million bits per second), but Internet protocol development is governed by the Internet Architecture Board, and the InterNIC (Internet Network Information Centre) administers the naming of computers and networks.

Amateur radio, cable television wires, spread spectrum radio, satellite, and fibre optics all have been used to deliver Internet services. Networked games, networked monetary transactions, and virtual museums are among applications being developed that both extend the network's utility and test the limits of its technology.

ANDREAS SOFRONIOU

4. THE INTERNET NOW

4.1 WEB SERVERS

The other major approach to client-server communications is via the World Wide Web. Web servers may be accessed over the Internet from almost any hardware platform with client applications known as Web browsers. In this architecture, clients need few capabilities beyond Web browsing (the simplest such clients are known as network machines and are analogous to simple computer terminals). This is because the Web server can hold all of the desired applications and handle all of the requisite computations, with the client's role limited to supplying input and displaying the server-generated output. This approach to the implementation of, for example, business systems for large enterprises with hundreds or even thousands of clients is likely to become increasingly common in the future.

4.2 INTERNET NETWORKING

The Internet is a massive network of networks, a networking infrastructure. It connects millions of computers together globally, forming a network in which any computer can communicate with any other computer as long as they are both connected to the Internet. Information that travels over the Internet does so via a variety of languages known as protocols.

4.3 ACCESSING INFORMATION

The World Wide Web, or simply Web, is a way of accessing information over the medium of the Internet. It is an information-sharing model that is built on top of the Internet. The Web uses the HTTP protocol, only one of the languages spoken over the Internet, to transmit data. Web services, which use HTTP to allow applications to communicate in order to exchange business logic, use the Web to share information. The Web also utilizes browsers, such as Internet Explorer or Firefox, to access Web documents called Web pages that are linked to each other via hyperlinks. Web documents also contain graphics, sounds, text and video.

38

SURFING THE INTERNET
THEN, NOW, LATER.

The Web is just one of the ways that information can be disseminated over the Internet. The Internet, not the Web, is also used for e-mail, which relies on SMTP, Usenet news groups, instant messaging and FTP. So the Web is just a portion of the Internet, albeit a large portion, but the two terms are not synonymous and should not be confused.

4.4 WORLD WIDE WEB

(WWW), byname THE WEB, is the leading information retrieval service of the Internet (the worldwide computer network). The Web gives users access to a vast array of documents that are connected to each other by means of hypertext or hypermedia links--i.e., hyperlinks, electronic connections that link related pieces of information in order to allow a user easy access to them. Hypertext allows the user to select a word from text and thereby access other documents that contain additional information pertaining to that word; hypermedia documents feature links to images, sounds, animations, and movies.

The Web operates within the Internet's basic client-server format; servers are computer programs that store and transmit documents to other computers on the network when asked to, while clients are programs that request documents from a server as the user asks for them. Browser software allows users to view the retrieved documents.

4.5 HYPERTEXT MARKUP LANGUAGE (HTML)

A hypertext document with its corresponding text and hyperlinks is written in HyperText Markup Language (HTML) and is assigned an online address called a Uniform Resource Locator (URL).

The development of the World Wide Web was begun in 1989 by Tim Berners-Lee and his colleagues at CERN, an international scientific organization based in Geneva. They created a protocol, HyperText Transfer Protocol (HTTP), which standardized communication between servers and clients. Their text-based Web browser was made available for general release in January 1992.

ANDREAS SOFRONIOU

4.6 RAPID ACCEPTANCE

The World Wide Web gained rapid acceptance with the creation of a Web browser called Mosaic, which was developed in the United States by Marc Andreessen and others at the National Centre for Supercomputing Applications at the University of Illinois and was released in September 1993. Mosaic allowed people using the Web to use the same sort of "point-and-click" graphical manipulations that had been available in personal computers for some years. In April 1994 Andreessen co-founded Netscape Communications Corporation, whose Netscape Navigator became the dominant Web browser soon after its release in December 1994. By the mid-1990s the World Wide Web had millions of active users.

4.7 INTERNET OWNERSHIP

No one actually owns the Internet, and no single person or organization controls the Internet in its entirety.

The Internet is more of a concept than an actual tangible entity, and it relies on a physical infrastructure that connects networks to other networks.

There are many organizations, corporations, governments, schools, private citizens and service providers that all own pieces of the infrastructure, but there is no one body that owns it all. There are, however, organizations that oversee and standardize what happens on the Internet and assign IP addresses and domain names, such as the National Science Foundation, the Internet Engineering Task Force, ICANN, InterNIC and the Internet Architecture Board.

4.8 E-MAIL

Electronic mail (e-mail) is used for the sending of messages via computer systems. Many computer systems are now connected to local or wide-area networks and users can communicate with other users anywhere on the network. Some services offer facilities that allow users to send and receive messages via a microcomputer, a telephone, and a modem. The sender and receiver need not be on-line at the time; the message is held in a computer mail-box, which the receiver is able to access.

4.9 E-MAILS BOUNCE

In computer jargon, a bounced e-mail is one that never arrives in the recipient's inbox and is sent back, or bounced back, to the sender with an error message that indicates to the sender that the e-mail was never successfully transmitted.

When a user attempts to send an e-mail, he is telling his e-mail system to look for the domain of the recipient and the domain's mail server. Once the e-mail system makes contact with the recipient's mail server, the mail server looks at the message to determine if it will let the message pass through the server. If the recipient's server has predetermined that it is not accepting e-mails from the sender's address the server will reject the message and it will subsequently bounce back to the sender. The message will also bounce back to the server if the mail server on the recipient's end is busy and cannot handle the request at that time. When an e-mail is returned to the sender without being accepted by the recipient's mail server, this is called a hard bounce.

Once the e-mail has been accepted by the recipient's mail server there are still ways for the message to be rejected. The mail server has to determine if the recipient actually exists within its system and if that recipient is allowed to accept e-mails. If the recipient's address does not exist on the mail server, then the message will be rejected because there is no one to deliver the message to. If the sender misspells the recipient's address then the system will recognize this as a non-existent address and bounce the message back. If the recipient exists but does not have enough disk space to accept the message then the message will bounce back to the sender.

Some mail systems predetermine a maximum message size that it will accept and will automatically bounce the message if it exceeds that size and some mail systems predetermine a maximum amount of disk space the user is allowed to occupy on the server. When an e-mail is returned to the sender after it has already been accepted by the recipient's mail server, this is called a soft bounce. Some mail servers are programmed to accept incoming e-mails and store them for further analysis without initially checking to determine if the recipient exists or is even capable of receiving the message.

41

Occasionally, a network failure at the sender or recipient end will cause an e-mail to bounce back to the sender. Typically, a bounced e-mail returns to the sender with an explanation of why the message bounced

4.10 INTERNET OWNERSHIP DEBATED

It is true that the Internet is distributed, so that bringing down one part of it does not disrupt the entire network, but it is definitely controlled by someone. The core system that makes the Internet function, in fact, is run by a U.S. entity known as ICANN , the Internet Corporation for Assigned Names and Numbers, which basically holds the keys for any person or business hoping to turn up in search results on the Internet.

The Internet DNS in turn is based on a system of "root servers," each of which carries a copy of all the IP addresses in a given section of the Internet and the Websites they point to.

The system of root servers and the administration of "top-level domains" (such as .com, .net, and .org) and the various country domains (such as .us, .ca, or .de) is overseen by ICANN. Another agency, the Internet Assigned Numbers Authority (IANA), is charged with technically handling and supporting the DNS and root servers. IANA is controlled by ICANN.

At one point in 2005, a movement emerged that was aimed at transferring control over the DNS and the root servers to the United Nations. Critics were (and in many cases still are) upset by the fact that 10 of the 13 root servers are in the U.S., and that the one that is arguably most important, known as server A -- which administers the .com domain -- is controlled by a for-profit corporation called Verisign Inc. (Nasdaq: VRSN).

Several years ago, China was rumoured to be setting up its own alternate domain system with root servers under its own control, because it was reportedly concerned about U.S. dominance over the Internet. But as it turned out, the country seems to have just added its own layer of addresses on top of the existing ICANN ones, forcing Chinese ISPs to translate the new top-level domains and map them to existing tables of U.S. names.

42

Whether it is actually controlled by the U.S. or not, the ICANN/IANA system has evolved to the point where everyone is used to it and the system effectively can't function without these agencies.

So even countries like China have to play ball -- whether they like it or not

4.11 DOMAINS

Domain name on internet is like real estate on the planet. Not that it is capped, like our planet's real estate, but it is still a scarce resource. Though its supply keeps increasing (addition of new domains like .tv, .info, .biz, etc.) but the adoption rate of new domains is painfully slow. So conventional economics (and thus the pricing) comes into play when it comes to its allocation like allocation of any other scarce resource. So while hosting got free & remains free due to abundant supply, second level domains (like YOU.com) never got free.

.com/.net/.org are international domains, but the similar TLDs .gov & .mil are not. .US was supposed to be the one to be used by US enterprises, but this never picked off. It is used by U.S. State and local governments. This made .com continue serving both as US as well as International one. And thus more pressure on .com domain.

Getting money out of innovation is not bad in itself; otherwise there will be little incentive to innovate. What is bad is the exploitation arising from innovation. It is just that the regulator should intervene at the right time to promote openness and adoption in larger public interest and curtailing/limiting profitably. But this should be done at the right time. So far this is no problem when the authorising agencies continue to be benevolent, regulator remains vigilant and consumers are aware.

So as far as the control over domain names is concerned I would not term it as controlled. I would label it as regulated & moderated & also partly-paid-for so that incentives for quality as well as innovation remain there.

4.12 INTERNET CONTRIBUTORS

So many people have made major contributions to the field of computer and Internet technology and just as many were involved in the development of the internet; it would be an impossible task to list all.

Some are computer scientists whose developments have paved the way for the Internet of today; some are founders of companies that have influenced the direction of new developments and e-commerce trends. The one thing they all have in common is that the Internet would not be what it is today without the work they have done. As the technology leaps forward at a rapid pace, the list will continue to grow as new innovators make their mark on the industry. We realize that there are hundreds of people who have shaped the industry, and we strongly encourage our readers to submit the name of any person that deserves to be included in our list.

When we talk about the Internet, we talk about the World Wide Web from the past four or five years. But, its history goes back a lot further; all the way back to the 1950s and 60s. When America was so fascinated with sending men into outer space, hundreds of miles away; it never saw what was being invented to bring everyone closer together, eventually.

4.13 GLOBAL SYSTEM

The Internet is a global system of interconnected computer networks that use the standard Internet protocol suite (TCP/IP) to serve several billion users worldwide. It is a network of networks that consists of millions of private, public, academic, business, and government networks, of local to global scope, that are linked by a broad array of electronic, wireless, and optical networking technologies. The Internet carries an extensive range of information resources and services, such as the inter-linked hypertext documents of the World Wide Web (WWW), the infrastructure to support email, and peer-to-peer networks.

The origins of the Internet date back to research commissioned by the United States government in the 1960s to build robust, fault-tolerant communication via computer networks. While this work, together with work in the United Kingdom and France, led to important precursor networks, they were not the Internet. There is no consensus on the exact date when the modern Internet came into being, but sometime in the early to mid-1980s is considered reasonable.

4.14 FUNDING

The funding of a new U.S. backbone by the National Science Foundation in the 1980s, as well as private funding for other commercial backbones, led to worldwide participation in the development of new networking technologies, and the merger of many networks. Though the Internet has been widely used by academia since the 1980s, the commercialization of what was by the 1990s an international network resulted in its popularization and incorporation into virtually every aspect of modern human life. As of June 2012, more than 2.4 billion people — over a third of the world's human population — have used the services of the Internet; approximately 100 times more people than were using it in 1995. Internet use grew rapidly in the West from the mid-1990s to early 2000s and from the late 1990s to present in the developing world. In 1994 only 3% of American classrooms had the Internet while by 2002 92% did.

4.15 TRADITIONAL COMMUNICATIONS MEDIA

Most traditional communications media including telephone, music, film, and television are being reshaped or redefined by the Internet, giving birth to new services such as voice over Internet Protocol (VoIP) and Internet Protocol television (IPTV). Newspaper, book, and other print publishing are adapting to website technology, or are reshaped into blogging and web feeds. The Internet has enabled and accelerated new forms of human interactions through instant messaging, Internet forums, and social networking. Online shopping has boomed both for major retail outlets and small artisans and traders. Business-to-business and financial services on the Internet affect supply chains across entire industries.

45

4.16 NON-CENTRALIZED GOVERNANCE

The Internet has no centralized governance in either technological implementation or policies for access and usage; each constituent network sets its own policies. Only the overreaching definitions of the two principal name spaces in the Internet, the Internet Protocol address space and the Domain Name System, are directed by a maintainer organization, the Internet Corporation for Assigned Names and Numbers (ICANN). The technical underpinning and standardization of the core protocols (IPv4 and IPv6) is an activity of the Internet Engineering Task Force (IETF), a non-profit organization of loosely affiliated international participants that anyone may associate with by contributing technical expertise.

5. WORLD WIDE WEB

5.1 THE WEB

The World Wide Web (abbreviated as WWW or W3, commonly known as the web) is a system of interlinked hypertext documents accessed via the Internet. With a web browser, one can view web pages that may contain text, images, videos, and other multimedia and navigate between them via hyperlinks.

In March 1989 Tim Berners-Lee, a British computer scientist and former CERN employee, wrote a proposal for what would eventually become the World Wide Web. The 1989 proposal was meant for a more effective CERN communication system but Berners-Lee eventually realised the concept could be implemented throughout the world. Berners-Lee and Belgian computer scientist Robert Cailliau proposed in 1990 to use hypertext "to link and access information of various kinds as a web of nodes in which the user can browse at will", and Berners-Lee finished the first website in December of that year. Berners-Lee posted the project on the alt.hypertext newsgroup on 7 August 1991

5.2 ACCUMULATED KNOWLEDGE

In the May 1970 issue of 'In March 1989, Tim Berners-Lee wrote a proposal that referenced ENQUIRE, a database and software project he had built in 1980, and described a more elaborate information management system. 'Popular Science magazine, Arthur C. Clarke predicted that satellites would someday "bring the accumulated knowledge of the world to your fingertips" using a console that would combine multi-functionality.

Tim Berners-Lee wrote a proposal that referenced ENQUIRE, a database and software project he had built in 1980, and described a more elaborate information management system, a formal proposal (on 12 November 1990) to build a "Hypertext project" called "WorldWideWeb" (one word, also "W3") as a "web" of "hypertext documents" to be viewed by "browsers" using a client–server architecture.

This proposal estimated that a read-only web would be developed within three months and that it would take six months to achieve "the

47

creation of new links and new material by readers, [so that] authorship becomes universal".

5.3 THE CERN DATA CENTRE

A NeXT Computer was used by Berners-Lee as the world's first web server and also to write the first web browser, WorldWideWeb, in 1990. By Christmas 1990, Berners-Lee had built all the tools necessary for a working Web: the first web browser (which was a web editor as well); the first web server; and the first web pages, which described the project itself.

The first web page may be lost, but Paul Jones (computer technologist) of UNC-Chapel Hill in North Carolina revealed in May 2013 that he has a copy of a page given to him by Berners-Lee during a visit to UNC in 1991 which is the oldest known web page. Jones stored it on a magneto-optical drive and on his NeXT computer.

On 6 August 1991, Berners-Lee posted a short summary of the World Wide Web project on the alt.hypertext newsgroup. This date also marked the debut of the Web as a publicly available service on the Internet, although new users only access it after August 23. For this reason this is considered the internaut's day. Many news-media have reported that the first photo on the web was uploaded by Berners-Lee in 1992, an image of the CERN house band Les Horribles Cernettes taken by Silvano de Gennaro; Gennaro has disclaimed this story, writing that media were "totally distorting our words for the sake of cheap sensationalism."

The first server outside Europe was set up at the Stanford Linear Accelerator Centre (SLAC) in Palo Alto, California, to host the SPIRES-HEP database. Accounts differ substantially as to the date of this event. The World Wide Web Consortium says December 1992, whereas SLAC itself claims 1991. This is supported by a W3C document titled A Little History of the World Wide Web.

5.4 CONCEPT OF HYPERTEXT

The crucial underlying concept of hypertext originated with older projects from the 1960s, such as the Hypertext Editing System (HES) at Brown University, Ted Nelson's Project Xanadu, and Douglas Engelbart's oN-Line System (NLS). Both Nelson and Engelbart were in

48

turn inspired by Vannevar Bush's microfilm-based "memex", which was described in the 1945 essay "As We May Think".

Berners-Lee's breakthrough was to marry hypertext to the Internet. In his book Weaving The Web, he explains that he had repeatedly suggested that a marriage between the two technologies was possible to members of both technical communities, but when no one took up his invitation, he finally assumed the project himself.

5.5 ESSENTIAL TECHNOLOGIES

In the process, he developed three essential technologies:

- a system of globally unique identifiers for resources on the Web and elsewhere, the universal document identifier (UDI), later known as uniform resource locator (URL) and uniform resource identifier (URI);

- the publishing language HyperText Markup Language (HTML);

- the Hypertext Transfer Protocol (HTTP).[30]

The World Wide Web had a number of differences from other hypertext systems available at the time. The web required only unidirectional links rather than bidirectional ones, making it possible for someone to link to another resource without action by the owner of that resource.

It also significantly reduced the difficulty of implementing web servers and browsers (in comparison to earlier systems), but in turn presented the chronic problem of link rot. Unlike predecessors such as HyperCard, the World Wide Web was non-proprietary, making it possible to develop servers and clients independently and to add extensions without licensing restrictions.

On 30 April 1993, CERN announced that the World Wide Web would be free to anyone, with no fees due. Coming two months after the announcement that the server implementation of the Gopher protocol was no longer free to use, this produced a rapid shift away from Gopher and towards the Web. An early popular web browser was ViolaWWW for Unix and the X Windowing System.

Robert Cailliau, Jean-François Abramatic of IBM, and Tim Berners-Lee at the 10th anniversary of the World Wide Web Consortium.

5.6 TURNING POINT

Scholars generally agree that a turning point for the World Wide Web began with the introduction of the Mosaic web browser in 1993, a graphical browser developed by a team at the National Centre for Supercomputing Applications at the University of Illinois at Urbana-Champaign (NCSA-UIUC), led by Marc Andreessen. Funding for Mosaic came from the U.S. High-Performance Computing and Communications Initiative and the High Performance Computing and Communication Act of 1991, one of several computing developments initiated by U.S. Senator Al Gore.[34] Prior to the release of Mosaic, graphics were not commonly mixed with text in web pages and the web's popularity was less than older protocols in use over the Internet, such as Gopher and Wide Area Information Servers (WAIS). Mosaic's graphical user interface allowed the Web to become, by far, the most popular Internet protocol.

The World Wide Web Consortium (W3C) was founded by Tim Berners-Lee after he left the European Organization for Nuclear Research (CERN) in October 1994. It was founded at the Massachusetts Institute of Technology Laboratory for Computer Science (MIT/LCS) with support from the Defence Advanced Research Projects Agency (DARPA), which had pioneered the Internet; a year later, a second site was founded at INRIA (a French national computer research lab) with support from the European Commission DG InfSo; and in 1996, a third continental site was created in Japan at Keio University.

By the end of 1994, while the total number of websites was still minute compared to present standards, quite a number of notable websites were already active, many of which are the precursors or inspiration for today's most popular services.

5.7 INTERNATIONAL STANDARDS

Connected by the existing Internet, other websites were created around the world, adding international standards for domain names and HTML. Since then, Berners-Lee has played an active role in guiding the development of web standards (such as the mark-up languages in which web pages are composed), and has advocated his vision of a Semantic Web. The World Wide Web enabled the spread of information over the Internet through an easy-to-use and flexible format. It thus played an important role in popularizing use of the Internet. Although the two terms are sometimes conflated in popular use, World Wide Web is not synonymous with Internet. The web is a collection of documents and both client and server software using Internet protocols such as TCP/IP and HTTP.

Tim Berners-Lee was knighted in 2004 by Queen Elizabeth II for his contribution to the World Wide Web.

5.8 FUNCTION

The terms Internet and World Wide Web are often used in everyday speech without much distinction. However, the Internet and the World Wide Web are not the same. The Internet is a global system of interconnected computer networks. In contrast, the web is one of the services that run on the Internet. It is a collection of text documents and other resources, linked by hyperlinks and URLs, usually accessed by web browsers from web servers. In short, the web can be thought of as an application "running" on the Internet.

Viewing a web page on the World Wide Web normally begins either by typing the URL of the page into a web browser or by following a hyperlink to that page or resource. The web browser then initiates a series of communication messages, behind the scenes, in order to fetch and display it. In the 1990s, using a browser to view web pages — and to move from one web page to another through hyperlinks — came to be known as 'browsing,' 'web surfing,' or 'navigating the web'. Early studies of this new behaviour investigated user patterns in using web browsers. One study, for example, found five user patterns: exploratory surfing, window surfing, evolved surfing, bounded navigation and targeted navigation.

The following example demonstrates how a web browser works. Consider accessing a page with the URL http://example.org/wiki/World_Wide_Web.

First, the browser resolves the server-name portion of the URL (example.org) into an Internet Protocol address using the globally distributed database known as the Domain Name System (DNS); this lookup returns an IP address such as 208.80.152.2. The browser then requests the resource by sending an HTTP request across the Internet to the computer at that particular address. It makes the request to a particular application port in the underlying Internet Protocol Suite so that the computer receiving the request can distinguish an HTTP request from other network protocols it may be servicing such as e-mail delivery; the HTTP protocol normally uses port 80. The content of the HTTP request can be as simple as the two lines of text GET /wiki/World_Wide_Web HTTP/1.1 Host: example.org

The computer receiving the HTTP request delivers it to web server software listening for requests on port 80. If the web server can fulfil the request it sends an HTTP response back to the browser indicating success, which can be as simple as HTTP/1.0 200 OK Content-Type: text/html; charset=UTF-8 followed by the content of the requested page. The Hypertext Markup Language for a basic web page looks like <html> <head> <title>Example.org – The World Wide Web</title> </head> <body> <p>The World Wide Web, abbreviated as WWW and commonly known ...</p> </body> </html>

The web browser parses the HTML, interpreting the markup (<title>, <p> for paragraph, and such) that surrounds the words in order to draw the text on the screen.

Many web pages use HTML to reference the URLs of other resources such as images, other embedded media, scripts that affect page behaviour, and Cascading Style Sheets that affect page layout. The browser will make additional HTTP requests to the web server for these other Internet media types. As it receives their content from the web server, the browser progressively renders the page onto the screen as specified by its HTML and these additional resources.

5.9 LINKING

Most web pages contain hyperlinks to other related pages and perhaps to downloadable files, source documents, definitions and other web resources. In the underlying HTML, a hyperlink looks like <a href="http://example.org/wiki/Main_Page">Example.org, a free encyclopedia</a>

Graphic representation of a minute fraction of the WWW, demonstrating hyperlinks

Such a collection of useful, related resources, interconnected via hypertext links is dubbed a web of information. Publication on the Internet created what Tim Berners-Lee first called the

WorldWideWeb (in its original CamelCase, which was subsequently discarded) in November 1990.

The hyperlink structure of the WWW is described by the webgraph: the nodes of the webgraph correspond to the web pages (or URLs) the directed edges between them to the hyperlinks.

Over time, many web resources pointed to by hyperlinks disappear, relocate, or are replaced with different content. This makes hyperlinks obsolete, a phenomenon referred to in some circles as link rot and the hyperlinks affected by it are often called dead links. The ephemeral nature of the Web has prompted many efforts to archive web sites. The Internet Archive, active since 1996, is the best known of such efforts.

5.10 DYNAMIC UPDATES

JavaScript is a scripting language that was initially developed in 1995 by Brendan Eich, then of Netscape, for use within web pages. The standardised version is ECMAScript. To make web pages more interactive, some web applications also use JavaScript techniques such as Ajax (asynchronous JavaScript and XML). Client-side script is delivered with the page that can make additional HTTP requests to the server, either in response to user actions such as mouse movements or clicks, or based on lapsed time. The server's responses are used to modify the current page rather than creating a new page with each response, so the server needs only to provide limited, incremental information. Multiple Ajax requests can be handled at the same time, and users can interact with the page while data is being retrieved. Web pages may also regularly poll the server to check whether new information is available.

5.11 WWW PREFIX

Many hostnames used for the World Wide Web begin with www because of the long-standing practice of naming Internet hosts (servers) according to the services they provide. The hostname for a web server is often www, in the same way that it may be ftp for an FTP server, and news or nntp for a USENET news server. These host names appear as Domain Name System or (DNS) subdomain names, as in www.example.com. The use of 'www' as a sub-domain name is not required by any technical or policy standard and many web sites do not use it; indeed, the first ever web server was called nxoc01.cern.ch. According to Paolo Palazzi, who worked at CERN along with Tim Berners-Lee, the popular use of 'www' sub-domain was accidental; the World Wide Web project page was intended to be published at www.cern.ch while info.cern.ch was intended to be the CERN home page, however the dns records were never switched, and the practice of pre-pending 'www' to an institution's website domain name was subsequently copied. Many established websites still use 'www', or they invent other sub-domain names such as 'www2', 'secure', etc.[citation needed] Many such web servers are set up so that both the domain root (e.g., example.com) and the www sub-domain (e.g., www.example.com) refer to the same site; others require one form or the other, or they may map to different web sites.

5.12 SUB-DOMAIN

The use of a sub-domain name is useful for load balancing incoming web traffic by creating a CNAME record that points to a cluster of web servers. Since, currently, only a sub-domain can be used in a CNAME, the same result cannot be achieved by using the bare domain root.[citation needed]

When a user submits an incomplete domain name to a web browser in its address bar input field, some web browsers automatically try adding the prefix "www" to the beginning of it and possibly ".com", ".org" and ".net" at the end, depending on what might be missing. For example, entering 'microsoft' may be transformed to http://www.microsoft.com/ and 'openoffice' to http://www.openoffice.org. This feature started appearing in early versions of Mozilla Firefox, when it still had the working title 'Firebird' in early 2003, from an earlier practice in browsers such as Lynx. It is reported that Microsoft was granted a US patent for the same idea in 2008, but only for mobile devices.

In English, www is usually read as double-u double-u double-u.[citation needed] Some users pronounce it dub-dub-dub, particularly in New Zealand. Stephen Fry, in his "Podgrammes" series of podcasts, pronounces it wuh wuh wuh.[citation needed] The English writer Douglas Adams once quipped in The Independent on Sunday (1999): "The World Wide Web is the only thing I know of whose shortened form takes three times longer to say than what it's short for".[citation needed] In Mandarin Chinese, World Wide Web is commonly translated via a phono-semantic matching to wàn wéi wǎng (万维网), which satisfies www and literally means "myriad dimensional net", a translation that very appropriately reflects the design concept and proliferation of the World Wide Web. Tim Berners-Lee's web-space states that World Wide Web is officially spelled as three separate words, each capitalised, with no intervening hyphens.

Use of the www prefix is declining as Web 2.0 web applications seek to brand their domain names and make them easily pronounceable. As the mobile web grows in popularity, services like Gmail.com, MySpace.com, Facebook.com and Twitter.com are most often discussed without adding www to the domain (or, indeed, the .com).

5.13 SCHEME SPECIFIERS: HTTP AND HTTPS

The scheme specifier http:// or https:// at the start of a web URI refers to Hypertext Transfer Protocol or HTTP Secure respectively. Unlike www, which has no specific purpose, these specify the communication protocol to be used for the request and response. The HTTP protocol is fundamental to the operation of the World Wide Web and the added encryption layer in HTTPS is essential when confidential information such as passwords or banking information are to be exchanged over the public Internet. Web browsers usually prepend http:// to addresses too, if omitted.

5.14 WEB SERVERS

The primary function of a web server is to deliver web pages on the request to clients. This means delivery of HTML documents and any additional content that may be included by a document, such as images, style sheets and scripts.

5.15 PRIVACY

Every time a web page is requested from a web server the server can identify, and usually it logs, the IP address from which the request arrived. Equally, unless set not to do so, most web browsers record the web pages that have been requested and viewed in a history feature, and usually cache much of the content locally. Unless HTTPS encryption is used, web requests and responses travel in plain text across the internet and they can be viewed, recorded and cached by intermediate systems.

When a web page asks for, and the user supplies, personally identifiable information such as their real name, address, e-mail address, etc., then a connection can be made between the current web traffic and that individual. If the website uses HTTP cookies, username and password authentication, or other tracking techniques, then it will be able to relate other web visits, before and after, to the identifiable information provided. In this way it is possible for a web-based organisation to develop and build a profile of the individual people who use its site or sites. It may be able to build a record for an individual that includes information about their leisure activities, their shopping interests, their profession, and other aspects of their demographic profile.

5.16 MARKETING AND ADVERTISING

These profiles are obviously of potential interest to marketeers, advertisers and others. Depending on the website's terms and conditions and the local laws that apply information from these profiles may be sold, shared, or passed to other organisations without the user being informed. For many ordinary people, this means little more than some unexpected e-mails in their in-box, or some uncannily relevant advertising on a future web page. For others, it can mean that time spent indulging an unusual interest can result in a deluge of further targeted marketing that may be unwelcome. Law enforcement, counter terrorism and espionage agencies can also identify, target and track individuals based on what appear to be their interests or proclivities on the web.

5.17 SOCIAL NETWORKING

Social networking sites make a point of trying to get the user to truthfully expose their real names, interests and locations. This makes the social networking experience more realistic and therefore engaging for all their users. On the other hand, photographs uploaded and unguarded statements made will be identified to the individual, who may regret some decisions to publish these data. Employers, schools, parents and other relatives may be influenced by aspects of social networking profiles that the posting individual did not intend for these audiences. On-line bullies may make use of personal information to harass or stalk users. Modern social networking websites allow fine grained control of the privacy settings for each individual posting, but these can be complex and not easy to find or use, especially for beginners.

5.18 POSTING ONTO WEBSITES

Photographs and videos posted onto websites have caused particular problems, as they can add a person's face to an on-line profile. With modern and potential facial recognition technology, it may then be possible to relate that face with other, previously anonymous, images, events and scenarios that have been imaged elsewhere. Because of image caching, mirroring and copying, it is difficult to remove an image from the World Wide Web.

5.19 INTELLECTUAL PROPERTY

The intellectual property rights for any creative work initially rest with its creator. Web users who want to publish their work onto the World Wide Web, however, need to be aware of the details of the way they do it. If artwork, photographs, writings, poems, or technical innovations are published by their creator onto a privately owned web server, then they may choose the copyright and other conditions freely themselves. This is unusual though; more commonly work is uploaded to websites and servers that are owned by other organizations. It depends upon the terms and conditions of the site or service provider to what extent the original owner automatically signs over rights to their work by the choice of destination and by the act of uploading.[citation needed]

Some users of the web erroneously assume that everything they may find online is freely available to them as if it was in the public domain, which is not always the case. Content owners that are aware of this widespread belief may expect that their published content will probably be used in some capacity somewhere without their permission. Some content publishers therefore embed digital watermarks in their media files, sometimes charging users to receive unmarked copies for legitimate use. Digital rights management includes forms of access control technology that further limit the use of digital content even after it has been bought or downloaded.[citation needed]

5.20 SECURITY

The web has become criminals' preferred pathway for spreading mal-ware. Cyber-crime carried out on the web can include identity theft, fraud, espionage and intelligence gathering. Web-based vulnerabilities now outnumber traditional computer security concerns, and as measured by Google, about one in ten web pages may contain malicious code. Most web-based attacks take place on legitimate websites, and most, as measured by Sophos, are hosted in the United States, China and Russia. The most common of all mal-ware threats is SQL injection attacks against websites. Through HTML and URIs the web was vulnerable to attacks like cross-site scripting (XSS) that came with the introduction of JavaScript and were exacerbated to some degree by Web 2.0 and Ajax web design that favours the use of scripts. Today by one estimate, 70% of all websites are open to XSS attacks on their users.

5.21 PROPOSED SOLUTIONS

Proposed solutions vary to extremes. Large security vendors like McAfee already design governance and compliance suites to meet post-9/11 regulations, and some, like Finjan have recommended active real-time inspection of code and all content regardless of its source. Some have argued that for enterprise to see security as a business opportunity rather than a cost centre, "ubiquitous, always-on digital rights management" enforced in the infrastructure by a handful of organizations must replace the hundreds of companies that today secure data and networks. Jonathan Zittrain has said users sharing responsibility for computing safety is far preferable to locking down the Internet.

5.22 STANDARDS

Many formal standards and other technical specifications and software define the operation of different aspects of the World Wide Web, the Internet, and computer information exchange. Many of the documents are the work of the World Wide Web Consortium (W3C), headed by

Berners-Lee, but some are produced by the Internet Engineering Task Force (IETF) and other organizations.

Usually, when web standards are discussed, the following publications are seen as foundational:

- Recommendations for mark-up languages, especially HTML and XHTML, from the W3C. These define the structure and interpretation of hypertext documents.
- Recommendations for style-sheets, especially CSS, from the W3C.
- Standards for ECMAScript (usually in the form of JavaScript), from Ecma International.
- Recommendations for the Document Object Model, from W3C.

Additional publications provide definitions of other essential technologies for the World Wide Web, including, but not limited to, the following:

- Uniform Resource Identifier (URI), which is a universal system for referencing resources on the Internet, such as hypertext documents and images. URIs, often called URLs, are defined by the IETF's RFC 3986 / STD 66: Uniform Resource Identifier (URI): Generic Syntax, as well as its predecessors and numerous URI scheme-defining RFCs;
- HyperText Transfer Protocol (HTTP), especially as defined by RFC 2616: HTTP/1.1 and RFC 2617: HTTP Authentication, which specify how the browser and server authenticate each other.

5.23 ACCESSIBILITY

There are methods available for accessing the web in alternative mediums and formats, so as to enable use by individuals with disabilities. These disabilities may be visual, auditory, physical, speech related, cognitive, neurological, or some combination therein. Accessibility features also help others with temporary disabilities like a broken arm or the aging population as their abilities change.

The Web is used for receiving information as well as providing information and interacting with society. The World Wide Web

Consortium claims it essential that the Web be accessible in order to provide equal access and equal opportunity to people with disabilities. Tim Berners-Lee once noted, "The power of the Web is in its universality. Access by everyone regardless of disability is an essential aspect." Many countries regulate web accessibility as a requirement for websites. International cooperation in the W3C Web Accessibility Initiative led to simple guidelines that web content authors as well as software developers can use to make the Web accessible to persons who may or may not be using assistive technology.

5.24 INTERNATIONALIZATION

The W3C Internationalization Activity assures that web technology will work in all languages, scripts, and cultures. Beginning in 2004 or 2005, Unicode gained ground and eventually in December 2007 surpassed both ASCII and Western European as the Web's most frequently used character encoding. Originally RFC 3986 allowed resources to be identified by URI in a subset of US-ASCII. RFC 3987 allows more characters—any character in the Universal Character Set—and now a resource can be identified by IRI in any language.

5.25 STATISTICS

Between 2005 and 2010, the number of web users doubled, and was expected to surpass two billion in 2010. Early studies in 1998 and 1999 estimating the size of the web using capture/recapture methods showed that much of the web was not indexed by search engines and the web was much larger than expected. According to a 2001 study, there were a massive number, over 550 billion, of documents on the Web, mostly in the invisible Web, or Deep Web. A 2002 survey of 2,024 million web pages determined that by far the most web content was in the English language: 56.4%; next were pages in German (7.7%), French (5.6%), and Japanese (4.9%).

A more recent study, which used web searches in 75 different languages to sample the web, determined that there were over 11.5 billion web pages in the publicly indexable web as of the end of January 2005. As of March 2009, the indexable web contains at least 25.21 billion pages. On 25 July 2008, Google software engineers Jesse Alpert and Nissan Hajaj announced that Google Search had discovered one trillion unique URLs. As of May 2009, over 109.5 million domains operated. [Not in citation given] Of these 74% were commercial or other domains operating in the .com generic top-level domain.

Statistics measuring a website's popularity are usually based either on the number of page views or on associated server 'hits' (file requests) that it receives.

5.26 SPEED ISSUES

Frustration over congestion issues in the Internet infrastructure and the high latency that results in slow browsing has led to a pejorative name for the World Wide Web: the World Wide Wait. Speeding up the Internet is an ongoing discussion over the use of peering and QoS technologies. Other solutions to reduce the congestion can be found at W3C. Guidelines for web response times are:

- Second (one tenth of a second). Ideal response time. The user does not sense any interruption.

- Second. Highest acceptable response time. Download times above 1 second interrupt the user experience.

- 10 seconds. Unacceptable response time. The user experience is interrupted and the user is likely to leave the site or system.

5.27 CACHING

If a user revisits a web page after only a short interval, the page data may not need to be re-obtained from the source web server. Almost all web browsers cache recently obtained data, usually on the local hard drive. HTTP requests sent by a browser will usually ask only for data that has changed since the last download. If the locally cached data are still current, they will be reused. Caching helps reduce the amount of web traffic on the Internet. The decision about expiration is made independently for each downloaded file, whether image, style-sheet, JavaScript, HTML, or other web resource. Thus even on sites with highly dynamic content, many of the basic resources need to be refreshed only occasionally. Web site designers find it worthwhile to collate resources such as CSS data and JavaScript into a few site-wide

61

files so that they can be cached efficiently. This helps reduce page download times and lowers demands on the Web server.

There are other components of the Internet that can cache web content. Corporate and academic firewalls often cache Web resources requested by one user for the benefit of all. (See also caching proxy server.) Some search engines also store cached content from websites. Apart from the facilities built into web servers that can determine when files have been updated and so need to be re-sent, designers of dynamically generated web pages can control the HTTP headers sent back to requesting users, so that transient or sensitive pages are not cached. Internet banking and news sites frequently use this facility. Data requested with an HTTP 'GET' is likely to be cached if other conditions are met; data obtained in response to a 'POST' is assumed to depend on the data that was POSTed and so is not cached.

5.28 ELECTRONIC COMMERCE

Online open auction site, eBay, grew to more than 5 million members by 1999.

Businesses often deploy private networks (intranets) for sharing information and collaborating within the company, usually insulated from the surrounding Internet by computer-security systems known as firewalls. Businesses also frequently rely on extranets, extensions of a company's intranet that allow portions of its internal network to be accessed by collaborating businesses. Access to these extranets is generally restricted via passwords.

Several important phenomena are associated with e-commerce. The role of geographic distance in forming business relationships is reduced. Barriers to entry into the retail business are lower, as it is relatively inexpensive to start a retail Web site. Some traditional business intermediaries are being replaced by their electronic equivalents or are being made entirely dispensable. (For instance, as airlines have published fare information and enabled ticketing directly over the Internet, store-front travel agencies have declined.) Prices of commodity products are generally lower on the Web--a reflection not merely of the lower costs of doing electronic business but also of the ease of comparison shopping in cyberspace. A new form of corporate cooperation known as a virtual company, which is actually a network

ANDREAS SOFRONIOU

of firms, each performing some of the processes needed to manufacture a product or deliver a service, has flourished.

5.29 ELECTRONIC PUBLISHING

Electronic publishing is the publication of books, magazines, etc., in electronic form rather than on paper, so that the information is accessible with a computer. Electronic publications are typically distributed on CD-ROM and generally contain graphics, photographic images, sound, and video clips as well as text (see multimedia). Publishing on-line is also becoming increasingly important, especially for academic journals.

5.30 DIGITIZATION

Digitization is the production of information recorded as a succession of discrete units, rather than as continuously varying (analogue) parameters. Digital systems most often record information in binary code, using only two states: one and zero. Information such as a message or numerical data can be transmitted from a keyboard by coding the alphabet and other symbols digitally. A sound may also be recorded (magnetic tape or compact disc) or transmitted in digital form. The electrical signal, into which the sound is converted by a microphone, is analogue in form since the voltage is changing continuously with time, but if the signal is sampled at intervals, then each sample voltage can be coded as a binary number. For example, a 6-V signal would become 0110, or zero, pulse, pulse, zero. By frequent sampling the whole analogue signal can be represented in a digital form.

Images may also be digitized and held in computer-readable form. In a raster image, the picture is broken up into a rectangular array of pixels, each of which can be represented by a sequence of bits. There are numerous formats for the files holding raster images. In the simplest, a bit-map format, the file essentially contains sequences of bits, one sequence for each pixel. More commonly, some sort of compression is used. For example, if a large area of the picture is blue sky of the same colour, it is not necessary to repeat the bit sequence for every picture in this area. All that is needed is a representation of the correct shade of blue together with an instruction indicating how many

63

times it appears. Photographs and artwork can be digitized using a scanner.

Another type of image file is a vector file. In this, the file contains instructions for drawing and colouring certain shapes; for instance, "draw a rectangle with sides 2 and 3" or "draw a circle with radius 5". Vector files are not broken into pixels; they are "digitized" in the sense that the information is held in digital form. They are produced by graphics and computer-aided-design (CAD) programs and are generally smaller files than raster-image files. The digitization of images is particularly important in desk-top publishing and electronic publishing.

5.31 DATA PROTECTION

Data protection are the arrangements used to ensure that confidential information, and especially computerized information, is available only to people entitled to use it. The twin purposes are to maintain the confidentiality of personal information and business secrets, and to enable the subjects on whom information is stored to ensure its accuracy. Electronic methods for combating unauthorized access to computers are supplemented in many countries by legal requirements. Typically, people who hold information about others are obliged to register with a regulatory agency, to comply with its codes of practice and to permit individuals to check and correct their records. Wrongfully obtaining access to material may be a criminal offence.

5.32 INFORMATION SEARCHING AND RETRIEVAL

State-of-the-art approaches to retrieving information employ two generic techniques:

- Matching words in the query against the database index (key-word searching) and

- Traversing the database with the aid of hypertext or hypermedia links.

Key-word searches can be made either more general or more narrow in scope by means of logical operators (e.g., disjunction and conjunction). Because of the semantic ambiguities involved in free-text indexing, however, the precision of the key-word retrieval technique--

that is, the percentage of relevant documents correctly retrieved from a collection--is far from ideal, and various modifications have been introduced to improve it. In one such enhancement, the search output is sorted by degree of relevance, based on a statistical match between the key words in the query and in the document; in another, the program automatically generates a new query using one or more documents considered relevant by the user. Key-word searching has been the dominant approach to text retrieval since the early 1960s; hypertext has so far been largely confined to personal or corporate information-retrieval applications.

The exponential growth of the use of computer networks in the 1990s presages significant changes in systems and techniques of information retrieval. In a wide-area information service, a number of which began operating at the beginning of the 1990s on the Internet computer network, a user's personal computer or terminal (called a client) can search simultaneously a number of databases maintained on heterogeneous computers (called servers). The latter are located at different geographic sites, and their databases contain different data types and often use incompatible data formats. The simultaneous, distributed search is possible because clients and servers agree on a standard document addressing scheme and adopt a common communications protocol that accommodates all the data types and formats used by the servers. Communication with other wide-area services using different protocols is accomplished by routing through so-called gateways capable of protocol translation.

Several representative clients are shown: a "dumb" terminal (i.e., one with no internal processor), a personal computer (PC), and Macintosh (trademark; Mac), and NeXT (trademark) machines. They have access to data on the servers sharing a common protocol as well as to data provided by services that require protocol conversion via the gateways. Network news is such a wide-area service, containing hundreds of news groups on a variety of subjects, by which users can read and post messages.

Evolving information-retrieval techniques, exemplified by an experimental interface to the NASA space shuttle reference manual, combine natural language, hyperlinks, and key-word searching. Other techniques, seeking higher levels of retrieval precision and effectiveness, are studied by researchers involved with artificial intelligence and neural networks. The next major milestone may be a

65

computer program that traverses the seamless information universe of wide-area electronic networks and continuously filters its contents through profiles of organizational and personal interest: the information robot of the 21st century.

5.33 SEMANTIC CONTENT ANALYSIS

The analysis of digitally recorded natural-language information from the semantic viewpoint is a matter of considerable complexity, and it lies at the foundation of such incipient applications as automatic question answering from a database or retrieval by means of unrestricted natural-language queries. The general approach has been that of computational linguistics: to derive representations of the syntactic and semantic relations among the linguistic elements of sentences and larger parts of the document. Syntactic relations are described by parsing (decomposing) the grammar of sentences

For semantic representation, three related formalisms dominate. In a so-called semantic network, conceptual entities such as objects, actions, or events are represented as a graph of linked nodes.

"Frames" represent, in a similar graph network, physical or abstract attributes of objects and in a sense define the objects. In "scripts," events and actions rather than objects are defined in terms of their attributes.

Indexing and linguistic analyses of text generate a relatively gross measure of the semantic relationship, or subject similarity, of documents in a given collection. Subject similarity is, however, a pragmatic phenomenon that varies with the observer and the circumstances of an observation (purpose, time, and so forth). A technique experimented with briefly in the mid-1960s, which assigned to each document one or more "roles" (functions) and one or more "links" (pointers to other documents having the same or a similar role), showed potential for a pragmatic measure of similarity; its use, however, was too unwieldy for the computing environment of the day. Some 20 years later, a similar technique became popular under the name "hypertext." In this technique, documents that a person or a group of persons consider related (by concept, sequence, hierarchy, experience, motive, or other characteristics) are connected via "hyperlinks," mimicking the way humans associate ideas. Objects so linked need not be only text; speech and music, graphics and images, and animation and video can all be interlinked into a "hypermedia" database. The objects are stored with their hyperlinks, and a user can easily navigate the network of associations by clicking with a mouse on a series of entries on a computer screen. Another technique that elicits semantic relationships from a body of text is SGML

5.34 CONCURRENCY

Concurrency refers to the execution of more than one procedure at the same time (perhaps with the access of shared data), either truly simultaneously (as on a multiprocessor) or in an unpredictably interleaved manner. Languages such as Ada (the U.S. Department of Defence standard applications language from 1983 until 1997) include both encapsulation and features to allow the programmer to specify the rules for interactions between concurrent procedures or tasks.

5.35 HIGH-LEVEL LANGUAGES

At a still higher level of abstraction lie visual programming languages, in which programmers graphically express what they want done by means of icons to represent data objects or processes and arrows to represent data flow or sequencing of operations. As of yet, none of these visual programming languages has found wide commercial acceptance. On the other hand, high-level user-interface languages for special-purpose software have been much more successful; for example, languages like Mathematica, in which sophisticated mathematics may be easily expressed, or the "fourth generation" database-querying languages that allow users to express requests for data with simple English-like commands. For example, a query such as "Select salary from payroll where employee = Jones,' " written in the database language SQL (Structured Query Language), is easily understood by the reader. The high-level language HTML (HyperText Markup Language) allows nonprogrammers to design Web pages by specifying their structure and content but leaves the detailed presentation and extraction of information to the client's Web browser.

5.36 SPEECH RECOGNITION

Although the GUI continued to evolve through the 1990s, particularly as features of Internet software began to appear in more general applications, software designers actively researched its replacement. In particular, the advent of "computer appliances" (devices such as personal digital assistants, automobile control systems, television sets, videocassette recorders, microwave ovens, telephones, and even refrigerators--all endowed with the computational powers of the embedded microprocessor) made it apparent that new means of navigation and control were in order. By making use of powerful advances in speech recognition and natural language processing, these new interfaces might be more intuitive and effective than ever. Nevertheless, as a medium of communication with machines, they would only build upon the revolutionary changes introduced by the graphical user interface.

5.37 INTERNET RETAILING

In 1998 consumers could purchase virtually anything over the Internet. Books, compact discs, computers, stocks, and even new and used automobiles were widely available from World Wide Web sites that seemed to spring up almost daily. A few years earlier, sceptics had predicted that consumers accustomed to shopping in stores would be reluctant to buy items that they could not see or touch in person. For a growing number of time-starved consumers, however, shopping from their home computer was proving to be a convenient, cost-effective alternative to driving to the store.

The Massachusetts-based Forrester Research estimated that in 1998 U.S. consumers would purchase $7.3 billion of goods over the Internet, double the 1997 total, and the firm expected on-line sales to increase an additional 65% in 1999 to about $12 billion. Computers and software were the most frequent purchases, accounting for about one-third of all sales; travel services, compact discs, and books were also popular. Finding a bargain was getting easier, owing to the rise of on-line auctions, such as the increasingly popular eBay, and Web sites that did comparison shopping on the Internet for the best deal.

For all the consumer interest, retailing in cyberspace was still a largely unprofitable business, however. Internet pioneer Amazon.com, which began selling books in 1995 and later branched into recorded music and videos, posted revenue of $153.7 million in the third quarter, up from $37.9 million in the same period of 1997. Overall, however, the company's loss widened to $45.2 million from $9.6 million, and analysts did not expect the company to turn a profit until 2001. Despite gushing red ink, Amazon.com had a stock market value of many billions, reflecting investors' unbridled optimism about the future of the industry.

Internet retailing appealed to investors because it provided an efficient means for reaching millions of consumers without incurring the cost of operating brick-and-mortar stores with their armies of salespeople. Selling on-line carried its own risks, however. With so many companies vying for consumers' attention, price competition was intense and profit margins thin or nonexistent. In a demonstration of just how cutthroat the business had become, video retailer Reel.com sold the hit movie Titanic for $9.99, undercutting the $19.99 suggested retail price and losing about $6 on each copy sold. With Internet retailing still in its infancy, companies seemed willing to absorb such losses in a bid to establish a dominant market position.

Mergers and acquisitions were also common as competitors girded for the future. CDnow Inc. and N2K Inc., two of the largest on-line music retailers, agreed to merge, creating a formidable opponent to Amazon.com's compact disc business. Meanwhile, German media giant Bertelsmann AG agreed to buy 50% of Barnes & Noble Inc.'s on-line book business, providing yet another threat to Amazon.com.

5.38 ON-LINE POPULARITY

On-line use continued to grow in popularity throughout 1998. An IDC survey predicted that 23% of all U.S. households would be using an on-line service provider by the end of the year. The prediction was based partly on lower prices for PCs; the use of more hybrid PC-TV products, such as WebTV, which allowed TV users to surf some parts of the Internet; and the growing availability of high-speed cable modems. The potential for WebTV-like products was clear. At year's end AOL was said to be seeking a manufacturer of TV set-top boxes so that it could compete with Microsoft's WebTV product.

5.39 GAME CONSOLES

Yet another WebTV-related product emerged from an unlikely source. Sega, known for its computer game consoles, introduced in Japan its new Dreamcast game console, which would also function as a WebTV-like unit. Software to turn the game machine into a Web-browsing device was not expected to be available until mid-1999. In addition, Sony Corp., the leading competitor in home video-game machines, was expected to offer something similar in the future.

Retail sales on the Internet also increased as consumers began to take greater advantage of electronic commerce. On-line sales lived up to expectations during the Christmas holiday season. AOL reported a 350% increase in on-line shopping. Analysts estimated that more than two million households shopped on-line for the first time and that sales in the fourth quarter of 1998 would hit about $3.5 billion, as expected. That was almost three times the 1997 total. The unanswered question was how many of those holiday shoppers would become regular Internet buyers.

5.40 ENCRYPTION SOFTWARE

The running battle between the computer industry and the federal government over Internet encryption software continued, even though the federal government relaxed its export restrictions. Encryption, or encoding, software was intended to protect the privacy of on-line data transmissions and help safeguard business transactions. The software-encryption industry and some of its key customers had been battling the government for several years, claiming that encryption was important to the development of electronic commerce. In addition, American software companies had complained that export regulations made it difficult for them to compete in the world market for encryption. New rules from the Commerce Department allowed American firms to export products using the 56-bit Data Encryption Standard, the equivalent of an electronic lock with more than 70 quadrillion possible combinations. The government continued to limit exports of more powerful encryption software, although some could be sold in 46 countries to particular industries, such as insurance and health care. Despite relaxing export rules on encryption, the government continued to push for FBI access to computer-industry

70

encryption experts so that potential criminal activity on the Internet would not be protected from government scrutiny. The government promised it would place no limits on the export of encryption products for which the government was provided with codes, or keys, for reading the encrypted messages.

5.41 SCANDAL

In September the Internet played a role in the White House scandal of 1998. First it was chosen by Congress as the distribution medium for the text of Independent Counsel Kenneth Starr's report on his eight-month investigation into Pres. Bill Clinton's relationship with a former White House intern. Only days later it became one of the means of disseminating the video of Clinton's grand-jury testimony in the case. Because the streaming video technique used to deliver Clinton's testimony consumed much more bandwidth than the text-based report, there were concerns of gridlock on the Internet when many people tried to download the video at once. In the end the problem did not arise, because far fewer people downloaded the video than had downloaded Starr's report. The same news story helped boost the fortunes of the Internet's leading gossip columnist, Matt Drudge, who had helped break the White House scandal story in January by posting information on his Web site, the Drudge Report. Drudge, who had no journalistic training, maintained that the Internet opened up new opportunities for people who were not establishment journalists to present news information to a wide audience.

5.42 SYSTEMATIC EXCLUSION

The makeup of that wide Internet audience also became a concern in 1998 when a scientific study suggested that African-Americans were being systematically excluded from the on-line world. In April a study published in the journal Science reported that whites in the U.S. with annual household incomes below $40,000 were six times more likely than African-Americans to have used the World Wide Web within the previous week. Among low-income households, whites were found to be twice as likely to own a home computer as blacks. The study contended that because a smaller percentage of black households than white households had incomes of more than $40,000, computer access in the U.S. was being restricted to a smaller portion of the African-

71

American population than the white population. The Internet's role in rearranging American personal habits also was examined in 1998. A study showed that Americans were using the Internet to supplement TV news and newspapers, not to replace them, but it also found that 20% of Americans were going on-line at least once weekly to read the news, compared with 6% two years earlier.

5.43 DATA PACKETS

Long-distance telephone service over the Internet, once a technical curiosity, showed signs of becoming a real business in 1998. Several phone companies offered a service in which phone calls were transmitted digitally over the Internet at reduced rates. The Internet was designed to carry data packets, not voice calls, and adapting phone calls to the Net had resulted in some complaints of spotty voice quality. By year's end the service had improved to the point that Internet telephony could compete on the basis of its lower price. Typically the service sold for far less per minute than conventional long-distance service--largely because Internet telephony bypassed much of the conventional telephone switching network but also because Internet telephone service providers were exempt from some fees that conventional long-distance companies had to pay. In a few cases Net phone service was sold for a flat monthly rate that covered unlimited long-distance calling privileges. While relatively few cities were covered by the service, some companies were planning national service introductions by late 1998 or early 1999.

In the U.S. Congress several bills favourable to the computer industry were pending in late 1998. One would expand the ability of American companies to hire skilled foreign workers. Corporations wanted to be able to hire more foreign workers because of a shortage of technology workers in the country. Another bill would benefit firms that sold products over the Internet by giving them a three-year period in which they would not have to charge customers sales tax. During that time the government would devise a tax plan for Internet sales. Legislation also was pending that would create penalties for commercial Web-site operators who offered material considered harmful to minors. This legislation was opposed by the American Civil Liberties Union and some companies with Internet Web sites. Other U.S. government actions affected many public schools and libraries that had hoped for improved Internet access. They were to be beneficiaries of federal telecommunications reforms that allocated money for telecommunications services, Internet access, and some high-tech wiring costs. The subsidy turned out to be less than expected when the Federal Communications Commission (FCC), under pressure from Congress, cut funding for the program by 42% and shifted the emphasis to helping the nation's poorest schools and libraries. The FCC's cuts were made after Congress listened to complaints from long-distance telephone companies, which said they could not provide most of the $2,250,000,000 to fund the program without raising rates paid by their customers.

5.44 COMPUTER CRIME

Computer security continued to be a major concern as outside electronic attacks by computer "hackers" on government and business computers reached new heights, sparking investigations into who was responsible. Those investigations led to a number of arrests but underscored the vulnerability of many computer systems connected to the Internet. The Computer Security Institute, a non-profit research group in San Francisco, reported that 24% of corporations participating in its annual survey indicated that they had suffered an outside computer break-in within the previous year. About 44% said they had experienced incidents of unauthorized access to their computer systems by employees. In March a boy was charged in Massachusetts with having caused airport-control-tower computers to be out of service for six hours. The boy accomplished the task by wiping out telephone access to the airport's control tower.

The shutdown also affected the airport's fire department and security and weather services and the operations of several private airfreight firms. In April a Canadian man was arrested for having broken into a NASA Web site and caused more than $70,000 worth of damage. That same month the University of Minnesota was hit by a "smurf denial of service" attack on its computer systems, which shut down some computers, caused some data losses, and resulted in network slowdowns. (Such an attack floods the victim's computer network with replies to false tests of remote network computers.) In July two California teenagers pleaded guilty to juvenile delinquency charges after they accessed computers at the Lawrence Livermore National Laboratory and the U.S. Air Force. Although no classified computer systems were breached, the attack raised government fears because it

73

indicated the effectiveness of a well-organized and systematic hacker attack.

That same month flaws were discovered and corrected in two widely used E-mail programs that would potentially allow technically knowledgeable people to sabotage other people's PCs remotely. The unexpected flaws, which turned up in both Microsoft and Netscape E-mail programs, would enable an outsider electronically to crash or steal information from the computer that was using one of the affected programs.

5.45 PAEDOPHILES

In March more than 60 people were arrested as accused paedophiles who were trying to set up meetings with unsuspecting children over the Internet. New Hampshire police posed as children on the Internet to set up meetings with the accused adults (most of whom lived in northern Europe) and then arranged for them to be arrested. In September police in the U.S. and 11 other countries arrested more than 100 people in an international crackdown on the exchange of child pornography over the Internet.

A puzzling new computer virus struck near the end of the year, but experts were undecided about how big a threat it posed. Called the "Remote Explorer" virus, it was written by clever destruction-oriented programmers and was able to spread itself through corporate computer networks more rapidly than previously known viruses had. The virus attacked only computers using the Windows NT OS and only under certain conditions. Some experts said the virus had the ability to bring entire companies to a halt. It was unclear, however, whether the virus was a widespread phenomenon.

5.46 NETWORK SYSTEMS

Sun later sold many new and replacement network systems to the U.S. government. In 1986 Sun made its largest single sale of computers to a government agency when the National Security Agency signed an agreement for $500 million worth of Sun equipment.

Sun's engineers pioneered many important technologies adopted by the computer industry. In 1984 it released its Network File System software, which became a standard for computer file sharing across networks. In 1987 Sun became the first large computer company to use reduced-instruction-set computing (RISC) microprocessors in its primary product lines.

5.47 WINTEL COMPETITION

Despite its technical and financial strengths, the company faced growing competition in the 1990s from so-called Wintel machines-- computers running Microsoft Corporation's Windows NT operating system on Intel Corporation's Pentium microprocessors. Although Sun's equipment was generally much faster and more reliable than Wintel systems, it was more expensive and far more complex to operate. Wintel computers controlled more than 85 percent of the worldwide market share for desktop systems, but they had a much smaller share of the market for the more profitable high-performance workstation and server systems used in business and on the Internet. Sun generally sold well in the server market, where performance was usually more important than price.

5.48 MICROSOFT CORPORATION

Microsoft is the leading developer of personal-computer software systems and applications. The company also publishes books and multimedia titles, offers electronic mail services, distributes programming via the Internet, and manufactures computer pointing devices. It has sales offices throughout the world but does virtually all of its research and development at its corporate headquarters in Redmond, Wash., U.S.

In 1975 William H. Gates and Paul G. Allen, two boyhood friends from Seattle, converted BASIC, a popular mainframe programming language, for use on an early personal computer (PC), the Altair. Shortly afterward Gates and Allen founded Microsoft, deriving the name from the words "microcomputer" and "software." During the next few years they refined BASIC and developed other programming languages. In 1980 International Business Machines (IBM) asked Microsoft to produce the essential software, or operating system for its first personal computer, the IBM PC. Microsoft purchased an operating system from another company, modified it, and renamed it MS-DOS (Microsoft Disk Operating System). MS-DOS was released with the IBM PC in 1981. Thereafter, most manufacturers of personal

75

computers licensed MS-DOS as their operating system, generating vast revenues for Microsoft; by the early 1990s it had sold more than 100 million copies of the program and defeated rival operating systems such as CP/M, which it displaced in the early 1980s, and later OS/2. Microsoft deepened its position in operating systems with its Windows graphical command program, whose third version, released in 1990, gained a wide following. By 1993, Windows 3.0 and its subsequent versions were selling at a rate of one million copies per month, and nearly 90 percent of the world's PCs ran on a Microsoft operating system. In 1995, the company released Windows 95, which for the first time fully integrated MS-DOS with Windows and effectively matched in ease of use Apple Computer's Macintosh OS. It also became the leader in productivity software such as word-processing and spreadsheet programs, outdistancing long-time rivals Lotus and WordPerfect in the process

As a result, by the mid-1990s Microsoft, which became a publicly owned corporation in 1986, had become one of the most powerful and profitable companies in American history. It consistently earned profits of 25 cents on every sales dollar, an astonishing record; net income topped $2.1 billion in the company's fiscal year ending June 30, 1996. However, its rapid growth in a fiercely competitive and fast-changing industry spawned resentment and jealousy among rivals, some of whom complained that the company's practices violated U.S. laws against unfair competition. Microsoft and its defenders countered that, far from stifling competition and technical innovation, its rise had encouraged both and that its software had consistently become less expensive and more useful. A U.S. Justice Department investigation concluded in 1994 with a settlement in which Microsoft changed some sales practices that the government contended enabled the company to unfairly discourage OS customers from trying alternative programs. The following year, the Justice Department successfully challenged Microsoft's proposed purchase of Intuit, the leading maker of financial software for the PC.

Partly because of its stunning success in PC software, Microsoft was slow to realize the commercial possibilities of network systems and the Internet. In 1993 it released Windows NT, a landmark program that tied disparate PCs together and offered improved reliability and network security. Sales were initially disappointing, but by 1996 Windows NT was hailed as the likely standard for PC networking, challenging Novell's NetWare. Microsoft did not move into Internet

76

software until a new venture, Netscape, had captured the emerging market for Web browsers, a new class of programs that simplified the once-arcane process of navigating the World Wide Web. In a violent change of course, Microsoft began pursuing Netscape with imitative offerings, which in less than a year achieved sufficient acceptance to challenge Netscape's continued dominance of the Web. It dramatically expanded its electronic publishing division, created in 1985 and already notable for the success of its multimedia encyclopaedia, Encarta. It also entered the information services and entertainment industries with a wide range of products and services, most notably the Microsoft Network and MSNBC (a joint venture with the National Broadcasting Company, a major American television network).

5.49 COMPUTER NETWORK

This is also called NETWORK, two or more computers that are connected with one another for the purpose of communicating data electronically. Besides physically connecting computer and communication devices, a network system serves the important function of establishing a cohesive architecture that allows a variety of equipment types to transfer information in a near-seamless fashion. Two popular architectures are ISO Open Systems Interconnection (OSI) and IBM's Systems Network Architecture (SNA).

Two basic network types are local-area networks (LANs) and wide-area (or long-haul) networks. LANs connect computers and peripheral devices in a limited physical area, such as a business office, laboratory, or college campus, by means of permanent links (wires, cables, fibre optics) that transmit data rapidly. A typical LAN consists of two or more personal computers, printers, and high-capacity disk-storage devices called file servers, which enable each computer on the network to access a common set of files. LAN operating system software, which interprets input and instructs networked devices, allows users to communicate with each other; share the printers and storage equipment; and simultaneously access centrally located processors, data, or programs (instruction sets). LAN users may also access other LANs or tap into wide-area networks. LANs with similar architectures are linked by "bridges," which act as transfer points. LANs with different architectures are linked by "gateways," which convert data as it passes between systems.

SURFING THE INTERNET
THEN, NOW, LATER.

Wide-area networks connect computers and smaller networks to larger networks over greater geographic areas, including different continents. They may link the computers by means of cables, optical fibres, or satellites, but their users commonly access the networks via a modem (a device that allows computers to communicate over telephone lines). The largest wide-area network is the Internet , a collection of networks and gateways linking millions of computer users on every continent.

5.50 CONSUMER PROTECTION

The growing popularity of computers and the Internet led to numerous state policy and funding debates during 1997. Many states grappled with novel problems arising from Internet use, including privacy of medical records, gambling availability, and other issues.

All states moved to address the serious computer network problem that would result from the change from 1999 to 2000. To save money and space, most programming in the past few decades had used only the final two digits in the date; consequently, computers in 2000 would assume the date was 1900, which would throw state payments, receipts, and other functions into disarray. One consulting firm estimated that fixing the problem could cost upwards of $600 billion during the next few years. Nevada became the first state to address year 2000 liability concerns. A new Nevada law provided immunity to state and local governments "from any civil action . . . caused by a computer that produced, calculated or generated an incorrect date."

When several states objected, a congressional effort to bar states from imposing extra taxes on Internet commercial trans-actions was stalled in the federal government during the year. States also moved to protect tax revenue from Internet expansion by cracking down on interstate wine and liquor sales. By the year's end, 21 states prohibited direct shipping of wine, with Georgia, Kentucky, and Florida classifying direct shipment as a felony. At the end of 1997, nine state attorneys general announced they were initiating an antitrust investigation against the Microsoft Corp. for monopolizing the market for operating-systems software.

ANDREAS SOFRONIOU

SURFING THE INTERNET
THEN, NOW, LATER.

5.51 HOUSEWARES

The increased growth of retail super-centres and the impact of the Internet on how retailers and manufacturers marketed to consumers had a profound effect on the housewares industry in 1998. (See Retailing: Sidebar, below.)

In 1997 American consumers spent more than $58 billion on such items as cookware, small electronic appliances, heating and cooling equipment, cleaning goods, and personal-care products, representing a 6.1% increase over 1996. The average household spent $560 on housewares, a $38 rise over 1996. The largest increase in sales occurred in miscellaneous household appliances, which rose by 34.1%. A 14.1% increase in non-electric cookware and a 13.9% boost in closet and storage accessories were also noteworthy. Sales of smoke alarms continued to rise, though the 10.4% increase was substantially less than the 1996 huge surge in all home-safety equipment. Decreased sales occurred mainly in silver serving accessories (39.5%), window coverings (6%), and clocks (2.8%).

The impact of the Internet continued to reshape the housewares market and affected the approach to sales. Many power retailers--i.e., top discount stores and specialty stores--offered on-line retailing, and a few product manufacturers used the Internet to sell wares directly to consumers. Using current estimates, industry observers predicted that within 10 years households purchasing goods over the Internet would increase annually from 200,000 to 15-20 million. Other virtual retailers, including mail-order catalogues and television infomercials, made up 5% of domestic housewares sales.

5.52 NETSCAPE COMMUNICATIONS CORP

In January 1995 the company recruited James L. Barksdale, an executive experienced with raising capital for new companies in the telecommunications and overnight-delivery industries, to be its president and chief executive officer. In August 1995 Netscape's initial public stock offering created a sensation in financial circles: in its first day of trading, the 16-month-old company's shares more than doubled, giving it a market capitalization of $2.2 billion. The proceeds helped to fund a series of acquisitions of smaller developers, as well as joint ventures with such prominent technology companies as Oracle Corporation, General Electric Co., and Novell, Inc.

79

5.53 BROWSER ENHANCEMENTS

Meanwhile, Netscape continued to extend its line of server applications and to roll out Navigator upgrades, adding features such as electronic mail (E-mail) and news. In addition, Netscape added a plug-in interface, allowing other developers to create modules that expanded Navigator's capabilities; this "open-architecture" approach led in particular to a proliferation of plug-ins for digital audio, video, and animation. Netscape was among the first licensees of Sun Microsystems, Inc.'s Java programming language and virtual-machine technology. Sun and Netscape also collaborated to define JavaScript, a separate language designed to help nonprogrammers create dynamic, interactive Web sites.

These rapid-fire advances pushed Netscape to the forefront of the software world. Web developers scrambled to implement its latest innovations; users raced to download each new release of its browser. Leading computer manufacturers and Internet service providers (ISPs) rushed to conclude agreements, allowing them to bundle Navigator with their products. By June 1996 Netscape claimed that more than 38 million people were using Navigator, making it the most popular personal-computer application ever.

Moreover, Netscape's innovations were transforming its browser from a simple application into a platform on which other developers could build. Observers began to suggest that the browser could become computing's dominant user interface and development framework. Since this analysis implied a reduction in the distinctiveness and importance of operating systems, Netscape's meteoric ascent was widely seen as a challenge to Microsoft, whose control of DOS and Windows OS had made it the dominant force in personal computing.

5.54 SUN MICROSYSTEMS JAVA

McNealy was famous for his assertion that "the network is the computer," which epitomized Sun's approach to networking interoperability. In 1995 Sun introduced the Java programming language to overcome some of the problems associated with networking different manufacturers' machines, often running different operating systems. According to its supporters, Java was a "Write once, run anywhere" computer language, meaning that software written in Java would not have to be rewritten for each computer operating system. If it ran on a UNIX computer, it should also run on a Windows machine or a Macintosh through the use of a Java Virtual Machine (JVM). JVMs were shipped with UNIX, Windows, Macintosh, and other systems as well as with Internet browsers such as Netscape's Navigator and Microsoft's Internet Explorer. Such versatility made Java a popular language to use when writing applications for the World Wide Web and, to many observers, seemed to portend a diminishing importance for individual operating systems. However, in 1997, Microsoft released a JVM that was incompatible with other JVMs, in effect breaking the "Write once, run anywhere" promise of the program. In November 1998 a U.S. federal judge issued a preliminary injunction preventing Microsoft from distributing further copies of its version of Java.

Sun also developed Java to enable a return to simpler and cheaper terminal-like network devices, particularly for database inquiry systems--such as airline reservation systems, inventory control systems, and Internet television devices--but also for use in personal digital assistants and various automotive and household appliance interfaces as well. In 1998 Motorola, Inc., signed a license agreement with Sun to use Java in its pagers and cellular telephones. In response, Microsoft joined the competition with a smaller version of its operating system, Windows CE, for use in network devices and appliances.

5.55 SEARCHES FOR BROWSER

In the fall of 1995, Microsoft began an urgent campaign to turn toward the Internet. It started by licensing the browser code that Andreessen and his NCSA associates had written while students and it feverishly developed Internet Explorer, a browser that gradually caught up with Navigator in features and performance. Microsoft kept Explorer completely free, even for business customers, and moved aggressively to persuade computer makers and ISPs to bundle it instead of Navigator. By 1996 Microsoft was bundling Explorer with Windows OS, and they had begun the process of integrating Explorer directly into Windows.

As a result, Netscape's market share among browser users, previously estimated at over 80 percent, began to decline. In response, Netscape accused Microsoft of unfair business practices and filed a series of complaints with regulatory bodies; these efforts helped to persuade the

U.S. Department of Justice to undertake a broad investigation of Microsoft under antitrust statutes.

Netscape also placed a greater emphasis on sales of server applications and corporate services, and it released a new product, Communicator, which combined the Navigator browser with workgroup-collaboration features designed to appeal to corporate customers. Another initiative was the creation of Netcenter, an information and commerce service built around its heavily trafficked Web site.

In all these areas, however, Netscape faced entrenched competitors. In early 1998 it reported slowing growth and its first quarterly operating loss ever. In an effort to regain market momentum, it declared Navigator and Communicator completely free and even made the programs' source code available to other developers for customizing and enhancement.

5.56 NAVIGATOR AND INTERNET

Clark and Andreessen planned to further this popularization process and to capitalize on it by marketing a commercial-quality Web browser, Web-server software, development tools, and related services. In October 1994 the company made available on its Web site the first version of Navigator, their new browser. By utilizing the shareware distribution model of "try before you buy" (except in education, where the program was free), Navigator was an immediate success: over the following 12 months some eight million copies were downloaded. Because Navigator connected to Netscape's Web site by default (and later because of various services offered by the company), netscape.com became one of the busiest sites on the Web. From an average of approximately 1 million hits per day in February 1995, traffic rose to more than 125 million hits per day by November 1997. The browser was followed by several Web-server applications, including pioneering programs for electronic commerce and security.

The company's rise to prominence triggered a dispute with the University of Illinois, which had trademarked the Mosaic name and designated another company as master licensee for the NCSA Mosaic software. As part of an out-of-court settlement, Mosaic Communications changed its name to Netscape Communications.

6. THE INTERNET LATER

6.1 NET NEUTRALITY

The Federal Communications Commission is moving aggressively to see that the Internet remains equally open to all. Despite recent court setbacks, the rules proposed for adoption should achieve that goal.

The principle here is "net neutrality," the concept that those who provide Internet service treat all information equally. This was no big deal in the early days of the Internet, when there was little money to be made in manipulating content. Today, however, the stakes are higher, much higher. The big providers, such as Verizon and Time Warner, do not like neutrality. They want to be able to give preferred access to those who pay for that access. These entities would get their data transmitted faster and at higher quality.

It is hard to overstate the importance of net neutrality. What would happen to the next Facebook or Google if providers were able to shunt them into the slow lane in order to give preferred access to established companies that were paying for the privilege?

What if your provider has a certain political philosophy and gives preferred access to sites that share that philosophy?

With television you can always change the channel. It is not that simple with Internet providers. The FCC is hoping for success the third time around. Two previous efforts to establish rules have been struck down in the courts. Surprisingly, the most recent setback may actually have been a victory.

The Court of Appeals for the District of Columbia threw out rules to prevent deals for preferential access, saying the federal government did not have the right to treat Internet service providers as utilities. However, the court said the FCC had some basic authority "to promulgate rules governing broadband providers' treatment of Internet traffic."

If anything, the outcome increased the FCC's powers. Broadband companies would be subject to strict disclosure — another power upheld by the D.C. court — and would face greater enforcement if they did not perform as promised.

SURFING THE INTERNET
THEN, NOW, LATER.

"Preserving the Internet as an open platform for innovation and expression while providing certainty and predictability in the marketplace is an important responsibility of this agency," said Tom Wheeler, who took over the FCC in November and has made net neutrality a priority.

Consumer advocates greeted the new rules with cautious optimism, though they would prefer that the FCC re-classify Internet providers as common carriers, or utilities. That sounds like a recipe for another court setback. Wheeler believes the rules will prevent preferential access.

6.2 POLITICAL INTERFERENCES

Republicans in Congress and on the FCC continue to be hostile to net neutrality. Mike O'Rielly, a commissioner, says he fears the FCC will go on to regulate Internet content providers, which is hard to contemplate.

"No matter how many times the court says 'no,' the Obama administration (remains determined) to put government in charge of the web," said a statement from U.S. Rep. Upton of Michigan, chair of the committee that oversees the FCC, and Rep. Greg Walden of Oregon, leader of the technology subcommittee.

No one is talking about putting the federal government in charge of the Internet. What the FCC is trying to do is keep private companies from exerting control over the Internet to determine what one can receive through the provider.

Why is it that those who harp about control by the government, which is in the final analysis control by the people, have no problem with control by corporations with any duty aside to their shareholders?

Anyway, the FCC understands what its duty is. This time, the rules should stand up to court scrutiny.

6.3 THE FUTURE OF ULTRA-FAST INTERNET

While you were not looking, the internet got super fast. We are not talking Google Fibre fast, but talking Star Trek fast. Today, it is not just possible to download a movie in seconds. New technology makes it easy to download dozens of movies in fractions of a second. Fast is almost too slow a word to describe such speed.

The following are just a few of the new exciting discoveries that stand to fundamentally change the way that we connect. The future moves at lightning speed — assuming we let it get there.

6. 4 LASERS

Like all wonderful things, the future of ultra-fast internet hinges on lasers. Fibre optic cables transmit data on waves of light, and as laser technology improves, data transfer speeds get faster. Researchers at CalTech, for instance, just announced a new type of laser with exceptionally high spectral purity. That means that the laser is closer than ever to operating on a single frequency, and since light with a higher spectral purity can carry more data, this new laser will offer faster connection speeds.

How much faster? That is so far unclear. It will have a hard time competing with another recent invention from CalTech's neighbours to the north. Scientists at the Stanford Linear Accelerator Centre (SLAC) are perfecting laser technology that adds a third dimension to data transmission. Current fibre optic technology only operates on two dimensions, but by adding a twist and introducing a third dimension, they're able to eclipse existing connection speeds. Last year, a team from Boston University used a similar method to achieve speeds as high as 1.6 terabits per second. Compare that to Google Fibre, which while faster than the vast majority of connections in America is still only 1 gigabit per second.

SURFING THE INTERNET
THEN, NOW, LATER.

6.5 MICROCHIPS

Finding ways to make information travel faster through the tubes is just part of the battle. Crazy laser technology only yields high speeds if the machines on either end of the connection can handle them. Thanks to another very recent breakthrough, we now have a chip that can accommodate mind-bending amounts of data.

The chip comes from the fine minds at IBM, and it is terrifically tiny but profoundly powerful. More specifically, it is an analogue-to-digital converter (ADC) that will enable faster and more complex digital equalization across long distance fibre channels. How much faster? Again, Google Fibre clocks in at 1 gigabit per second. This new IBM chip enables connections as fast as 400 gigabits per second. That's about 5,000 times faster than the average connection in the United States.

6.6 PROTOCOLS

Another aspect of internet speed people do not often think about is the rules that govern how data is exchanged between computers. In a word: protocol. Optimizing these rules can yield faster connections without expensive chores like replacing hardware or improving infrastructure. A lot faster.

The best example in recent history is the new Flexigrid protocol. Whereas current connections tend to travel through the cable all by its lonesome, Flexigrid lays multiple signals over each other in a single cable. That means that data races towards its destination on parallel planes, allowing for exponentially faster transfer points. At risk of wearing out the question, one asks: How much faster? One recent test in the United Kingdom sent seven 200 gigabit signals on one "Alien Super Channel" and reached speeds as high as 1.4 terabits per second. At speeds like that, you can download all the movies pretty much instantly.

Advances are not just limited to those with fibre at their disposal; they extend to the large part of the world still dependent on copper phone lines. Under the current protocol standard, VDSL, their connections are limited to just over 100 megabits per second. Slow! But a new protocol called G.fast allows for high-speed DSL—like, 1 gigabit per second style high speed — through existing copper line. Unfortunately, it might interfere with the FM radio spectrum, but who listens to the radio any more anyways?

6.7 SERVERS

The piece of hardware needed to make the internet work is server technology. After all, the internet lives on servers! So if we can improve servers, we can improve how the internet works.

6.8 EXPANSION

But what if we did not improve servers and just got rid of them instead? A new European Union-backed project called PURSUIT wants to do just that. Instead of relying on static servers to store all of the internet's data, backers of this project want to figure out a way to distribute that load across all computers on a given network. Think of it as peer-to-peer sharing, on an internet-wide scale.

This would involve doing away with the idea of URLs (Uniform Resource Locators) in favour of so-called URIs (Uniform Resource Identifiers) to find data. That data would live in many different locations instead of just one, which would improve speed, efficiency, and reliability. Inevitably, that means not having a central server that could go down in the event of an attack or massive data load.

6.9 PROTECTING THE FUTURE OF THE INTERNET

In 2013 the issue of Internet privacy was thrown into the spotlight, with the revelations that some governments have actively sanctioned certain spy agencies to intercept user data. These actions clearly go against the internet's founding principles of openness and freedom.

These principles are part of why and how the Internet has grown into an incredible tool that continually changes lives and connects people around the world.

It is difficult to imagine how many of the last 30 years' worth of achievements in education, health, art and science would have been possible without the Internet to support innovation and share knowledge.

SURFING THE INTERNET
THEN, NOW, LATER.

It is natural that the Internet community has railed against the government sponsored intrusion. Indeed, some of the world's biggest technology companies have spoken on the need to protect the privacy of Internet users – Apple, Microsoft and Google are just some of the companies supporting the Global Government Surveillance Reform group.

They are calling on governments around the world to tackle this issue and reform current policies that leave the privacy of Internet users at risk from data monitoring.

6.10 PROTECTING YOUR OWN PRIVACY

Although privacy on the Internet is proving to be a challenging issue, there are some things people can do to protect themselves.

While it is true that individual citizens have limited resources, it is worthwhile for everyone to invest a little time to encrypt their data. This would mean that the resources required to monitor all citizens would increase exponentially and make the task of examining all Internet traffic far more difficult.

Think of it in this way: if everyone in the world drove around in armoured cars, a lot of effort would have to be spent breaking into each and every car, without any guarantee of there being anything inside worth taking.

Similarly, if everybody encrypts their data, it would help to deter others from the effort involved in monitoring and decrypting it. Of course, the ideal solution is still that the monitoring of user data itself ceases immediately.

It would be terrible if people were afraid to use the Internet because they thought their privacy would be violated.

After all, privacy should be cherished and respected. It is even counted as a fundamental human right in many countries. Over the last 30 years, society has benefited immeasurably from the Internet, which has helped break down barriers and bring people closer together.

We should never lose sight of the Internet's founding principles and ideals, and push stakeholders at every level to respect them. The Internet needs to continue to operate with as much freedom as possible to help increase innovation. Without trust and cooperation, the

Internet simply cannot function, and that would be detrimental to our global society.

6.11 THE FUTURE OF THE WORLD WIDE WEB

Attention must be paid to this dated TV advertisement. It is almost twenty years old, but the wide-eyed wonder smeared all over the phrase, "America Online can do all that!" This is emblematic of the ecstasy which accompanied the World Wide Web's mid-nineties boom.

The list of totally, like, awesome stuff that the web could do at its inception in 1993 or two years later in the above advertisement is not that far from what still makes it a wonderful resource for us today. Ordering gifts at short notice, booking cheap plane tickets and socialising with geographically distant people who share the same interests – we are enamoured of it all, though these things are no longer outlandish promises of productivity. They have become 'quote-idian'.

6.12 WEB'S NEXT CHANGES

The future, depending on which view one takes, is available in various shades of fantastic, terrifying and insane. The most immediate changes to the web one would likely notice are improvements in sheer pace. Broadband speeds of a gigabit or more have just started to become available to some US and UK web-fans through ventures like Google Fibre or, in Britain, Hyper-optic. Speeds of over 10 gigabytes are predicted to become normal, as are huge step-ups in mobile broadband. While improvements in bandwidth are certain, what is still in the realms of pure, fun speculation is how we will make use of these hypersonic speeds.

6.13 DATA STREAMS INCREASE IN VOLUME

While data streams continue to exponentially increase in volume, however, the Internet will also begin to be supported in new and interesting places. Like space, Vint Cerf, one of the original architects of the infrastructure upon which the World Wide Web itself is built, has been hard at work thinking of ways to expand the Internet far beyond the confines of our planet.

SURFING THE INTERNET
THEN, NOW, LATER.

NASA, back in 2008, was already experimenting with lasers that could theoretically beam data back and forth between Earth and Mars. It's technology like that (named Lasercom) which could play a key role in the foundations of an "Interplanetary Internet" of the future.

Even if the architecture of the web can be deployed to new frontiers, that is not to say that the ideals which accompanied its inception will follow. Right now, the digital is a battleground for rival governments and organisations that possess contrasting beliefs on how the Internet should be managed.

6.14 CENSORSHIP OF SOCIAL MEDIA

Recently, Vietnam banned the sharing of news stories on social media – a move which signals the latest in a long line of crackdowns on cyber freedoms in certain Asian countries. As The Economist noted, the developing global schism on web censorship and the rise of intrusion by regimes is rapidly forcing nation states to put their cards on the table and decide whether they want to be hands-off or hands-on when it comes to controlling citizens' access.

6.15 GEOGRAPHICAL DIVISIONS

As the debate on this issue rages, it seems fair to say that the future web will be more divided geographically. In an outlandish, worst-case scenario, there could even be a true structural split in which a group of disgruntled countries completely cordon themselves off from the larger global network. This is mirrored by the eerie news that Apple has patented technology for security services to disable its devices temporarily within a certain radius.

According to MIT professor Jonathan Zittrain, even the commercial ownership of technology has a direct impact on our freedoms. In his book, "The Future of the Internet: And How to Stop it," Zittrain writes of his concerns over, "bundled hardware and software that is created and controlled by one company."

"This," he argues, "will affect how readily behaviour on the Internet can be regulated, which in turn will determine the extent that regulators and commercial incumbents can constrain amateur innovation, which has been responsible for much of what we now consider precious about the Internet."

ANDREAS SOFRONIOU

6.16 SEMANTIC WEB

It would be much easier for the public to show interest in exciting new cloud services than to talk about TCP/IP architecture or the virtues of generative systems. It is not surprising, therefore, that the rapid development of products like Google Now or iCloud has been so fore-grounded both by tech companies and the press.

The predictive travel advice of a service like Google Now is a very significant glimpse of what is to come in terms of a semantic web that allows machines to work automatically for us – even predicting our needs and desires.

Perhaps the cloud services will one day be able to extract data from the Internet of Things one owns (such as; fridge, TV, shoes, etc.) and make predictions about your risk of a heart attack or stroke based on a continuous, comprehensive and real-time assessment of your lifestyle.

6.17 PERSONALISED FILTER BUBBLES

Even before such modelling and simulation becomes widespread, personalised filter bubbles could become commonplace. For this to happen, the customisation of Internet content would have to deepen so much that, in the future, everything you see on the web – from the wording of news stories to the accent of a YouTube video's voice-over – could be altered based on what algorithms know about you, your personality and your mood that day.

Start-up Gravity is currently working in a similar field and the BBC has tested the ability to live-edit radio scripts in order to tailor them for regional listeners. All of this suggests that a full range of content, from text to audio and video could be moulded around your likes and dislikes in future decades. This is online data-mining (on a massive scale) that would make such a thing possible.

6.18 ALTERNATIVE EXISTENCE

Finally, as technologies like virtual reality headsets and new tele-presence robots become more sophisticated, there is a possibility that those chunky gigabit connections will be put to use supporting truly immersive alternate existences in other bodies – either physical or virtual.

It is exactly that kind of scenario which is present in the 2009 Bruce Willis action thriller Surrogates. Although Surrogates seems to be a film about robotics, it is just as much about connectivity between human and robot surrogate. Can a data connection be created for your entire body and the electrical signals in your nervous system? Can your thoughts be transported wirelessly into a host bot that is stronger, healthier and more attractive than you?

We are already playing with the surrogate identities of social network profiles and people have recently experienced living for extended periods as tele-presences in bots. So in the future, will we be able to experience the data feed from some surrogate presence across the planet as though its eyes were our eyes; its ears our ears, and so on? If so, the need for video casts and live blogs might disappear completely. We would, through whatever vessel, be there to watch it ourselves.

Just think. Twenty years ago they thought email was cool!

END

SURFING THE INTERNET
THEN, NOW, LATER.

93

SURFING THE INTERNET
THEN, NOW, LATER.

ANDREAS SOFRONIOU

SURFING THE INTERNET
THEN, NOW, LATER.

SURFING THE INTERNET
THEN, NOW, LATER.

ANDREAS SOFRONIOU

SURFING THE INTERNET
THEN, NOW, LATER.

BIBLIOGRAPHY

(ALL BOOKS LISTED BELOW WERE WRITTEN BY ANDREAS SOFRONIOU)

1. I.T. RISK MANAGEMENT, ISBN: 978-1-4467-5653-9
2. SYSTEMS ENGINEERING, ISBN: 978-1-4477-7553-9
3. BUSINESS INFORMATION SYSTEMS, CONCEPTS AND EXAMPLES, ISBN: 978-1-4092-7338-7
4. A GUIDE TO INFORMATION TECHNOLOGY, ISBN: 978-1-4092-7608-1
5. CHANGE MANAGEMENT IN I.T., ISBN: 978-1-4092-7712-5
6. FRONT-END DESIGN AND DEVELOPMENT FOR SYSTEMS APPLICATIONS, ISBN: 978-1-4092-7588-6
7. I.T RISK MANAGEMENT, ISBN: 978-1-4092-7488-9
8. THE SIMPLIFIED PROCEDURES FOR I.T. PROJECTS DEVELOPMENT, ISBN: 978-1-4092-7562-6
9. THE SIGMA METHODOLOGY FOR RISK MANAGEMENT IN SYSTEMS DEVELOPMENT, ISBN: 978-1-4092-7690-6
10. TRADING ON THE INTERNET IN THE YEAR 2000 AND BEYOND, ISBN: 978-1-4092- 7577
11. STRUCTURED SYSTEMS METHODOLOGY, ISBN: 978-1-4477-6610-0
12. INFORMATION TECHNOLOGY LOGICAL ANALYSIS, ISBN: 978-1-4717-1688-1
13. I.T. RISKS LOGICAL ANALYSIS, ISBN: 978-1-4717-1957-8
14. I.T. CHANGES LOGICAL ANALYSIS, ISBN: 978-1-4717-2288-2
15. LOGICAL ANALYSIS OF SYSTEMS, RISKS , CHANGES, ISBN: 978-1-4717-2294-3
16. COMPUTING, A PRÉCIS ON SYSTEMS, SOFTWARE AND HARDWARE, ISBN: 978-1-2910-5102-5
17. MANAGE THAT I.T. PROJECT, ISBN: 978-1-4717-5304-6
18. CHANGE MANAGEMENT, ISBN: 978-1-4457-6114-5
19. MANAGEMENT OF I.T. CHANGES, RISKS, WORKSHOPS, EPISTEMOLOGY, ISBN: 978-1-84753-147-6
20. THE MANAGEMENT OF COMMERCIAL COMPUTING, ISBN: 978-1-4092-7550-3
21. PROGRAMME MANAGEMENT WORKSHOP, ISBN: 978-1-4092-7583-1
22. THE PHILOSOPHICAL CONCEPTS OF MANAGEMENT THROUGH THE AGES, ISBN: 978-1-4092-7554-1
23. THE MANAGEMENT OF PROJECTS, SYSTEMS, INTERNET, AND RISKS, ISBN: 978-1-4092- 7464-3
24. HOW TO CONSTRUCT YOUR RESUMÊ, ISBN: 978-1-4092-7383-7
25. DEFINE THAT SYSTEM, ISBN: 978-1-291-15094-0
26. INFORMATION TECHNOLOGY WORKSHOP, ISBN: 978-1-291-16440-4
27. CHANGE MANAGEMENT IN SYSTEMS, ISBN: 978-1-4457-1099-0
28. SYSTEMS MANAGEMENT, ISBN: 978-1-4710-4907-1
29. TECHNOLOGY, A STUDY OF MECHANICAL ARTS AND APPLIED SCIENCES, ISBN: 978-1-291-58550-6
30. EXPERT SYSTEMS, KNOWLEDGE ENGINEERING FOR HUMAN REPLICATION, ISBN: 978-1-291-59509-3
31. ARTIFICIAL INTELLIGENCE AND INFORMATION TECHNOLOGY, ISBN: 978-1-291- 60445-0
32. PROJECT MANAGEMENT PROCEDURES FOR SYSTEMS DEVELOPMENT, ISBN: 978-0-952-72531-2
33. SURFING THE INTERNET, THEN, NOW, LATER. ISBN: 978-1-291-77653-9

SURFING THE INTERNET
THEN, NOW, LATER.

AUTHOR'S OTHER BOOKS PUBLICATONS

MEDICINE & PSYCHOLOGY

34. MEDICAL ETHICS THROUGH THE AGES, ISBN: 978-1-4092- 7468-1
35. MEDICAL ETHICS, FROM HIPPOCRATES TO THE 21ST CENTURY ISBN: 978-1-4457-1203-1
36. THE MISINTERPRETATION OF SIGMUND FREUD, ISBN: 978-1-4467-1659-5
37. JUNG'S PSYCHOTHERAPY: THE PSYCHOLOGICAL & MYTHOLOGICAL METHODS, ISBN: 978-1-4477-4740-6
38. FREUDIAN ANALYSIS & JUNGIAN SYNTHESIS, ISBN: 978-1-4477-5996-6
39. PSYCHOTHERAPY, CONCEPTS OF TREATMENT, ISBN: 978-1-291-50178-0
40. PSYCHOLOGY, CONCEPTS OF BEHAVIOUR, ISBN: 978-1-291-47573-9
41. PHILOSOPHY FOR HUMAN BEHAVIOUR, ISBN: 978-1-291-12707-2
42. SEX, AN EXPLORATION OF SEXUALITY, EROS AND LOVE, ISBN: 978-1-291-56931-5
43. PSYCHOLOGY FROM CONCEPTION TO SENILITY, ISBN: 978-1-4092-7218-2
44. PSYCHOLOGY OF CHILD CULTURE, ISBN: 978-1-4092-7619-7
45. JOYFUL PARENTING, ISBN: 0 9527956 1 2
46. THE GUIDE TO A JOYFUL PARENTING, ISBN: 0 952 7956 1 2

EDUCATION & PHILOSOPHY

47. THERAPEUTIC PHILOSOPHY FOR THE INDIVIDUAL AND THE STATE, ISBN: 978-1-4092-7586-2
48. PHILOSOPHIC COUNSELLING FOR PEOPLE AND THEIR GOVERNMENTS, ISBN: 978-1-4092-7400-1
49. MORAL PHILOSOPHY, FROM SOCRATES TO THE 21ST AEON, ISBN: 978-1-4457-4618-0
50. MORAL PHILOSOPHY, FROM HIPPOCRATES TO THE 21ST AEON, ISBN: 978-1-84753-463-7
51. MORAL PHILOSOPHY, THE ETHICAL APPROACH THROUGH THE AGES, ISBN: 978-1-4092-7703-3
52. MORAL PHILOSOPHY, ISBN: 978-1-4478-5037-3
53. 2011 POLITICS, ORGANISATIONS, PSYCHOANALYSIS, POETRY, ISBN: 978-1-4467-2741-6
54. PLATO'S EPISTEMOLOGY, ISBN: 978-1-4716-6584-4
55. ARISTOTLE'S AETIOLOGY, ISBN: 978-1-4716-7861-5
56. MARXISM, SOCIALISM & COMMUNISM, ISBN: 978-1-4716-8236-0
57. MACHIAVELLI'S POLITICS & RELEVANT PHILOSOPHICAL CONCEPTS, ISBN:

SURFING THE INTERNET
THEN, NOW, LATER.

978-1-4716-8629-0

SURFING THE INTERNET
THEN, NOW, LATER.

AUTHOR'S PROFILE

Andreas Sofroniou is a Business Director and an Information Technology Executive with U.K., U.S.A., and international organisations, an Expert on Computing for the European Union, a Principal Adviser to British Government Departments, a retired U.K. London Harley Street Consultant Psychotherapist, a Life Fellow of the Institute of Directors and a published author.

As an author, Andreas Sofroniou's eighty-three books were published by PulishAmerica, Nielsen, Whitaker, PsySys, & lulu.com/sofroniou. The titles include: Social Sciences, Medical Sciences, Psychotherapy, Psychoanalysis, Psychology, Sociology, Philology, Philosophy, Epistemology, Politics, History, Management, Technology, Information Technology, Expert Systems, Artificial Intelligence, Fiction, and Poetry.

CAREER

During his varied career, Andreas held the positions of Chief Executive Officer, Programmes Director, Managing Director, Overseas Marketing Executive, Production and Inventory Manager, Group Senior Systems Consultant, European Systems Manager, and Principal Technical Adviser with the multi-national organisations of EDS, PsySys, International Computers Limited (ICL), Pitney Bowes, Plessey (GEC), Raychem (Tyco) and the Engineering Industry Training Board (EITB).

For five years, the Global Programmes Director/Manager for EDS (Electronic Data Systems), the largest outsourcing international organisation. For twenty years, the Managing Director of PsySys Limited. a consultancy responsible for the development of systems, management and people. Many of EDS and PsySys clients are international companies, software houses, European Union Commissions and British Government Departments.

EDUCATION

Andreas holds the degrees of Doctor of Philosophy (Psychology), Executive MBA, Doctor of Science (I.T.), and Doctor of Science (Medical Sciences). He is a Life Fellow of the Institute of Directors, Life Fellow of The Institute of Management and Technology and A Research Fellow (Life) of the American Biographical Institute.

Other studies included: Children's Art and Psychotherapy, Mental Illness/Mental Health and Advanced Psychological Topics.

Previously, a Chartered Member and Fellow of eighteen professional institutions for: Engineering, Systems, Computing, Complementary Medicine, Management, Production, Programming, Marketing, Petroleum, Data Processing, Psychotherapy, and Counselling.

AWARDS

For achievements in Systems Engineering, Psychology and Directing, Andreas' biographical records are included in the directory of 'Who's Who in the World', published by Marquis/Macmillan and for Leadership in other international biographical publications.

In January 2003, Andreas and PsySys Limited received the Achievement Award for twenty years of continued growth and client satisfaction.

In March 2004, Andreas received the EDS award for Distinguished Global Services with the Company.